Selling Food with Doordash: Your Comprehensive Handbook for Virtual Restaurant Success

TABLE OF CONTENTS

Chapter 1: Introduction - The Dawn of Virtual Restaurant Business

Chapter 2: Understanding DoorDash - A Comprehensive Guide

Chapter 3: Building Your Virtual Restaurant: Startup Essentials

Chapter 4: Navigating The DoorDash Platform: A Detailed Walkthrough

Chapter 5. Developing Your Menu: Attracting Customers through Gastronomy

Chapter 6: Winning with Photography: How to Showcase Your Food

Chapter 7. Food Preparation: Tips and Tricks for Efficiency and Quality*

Chapter 8. Pricing Strategies for Success: Finding the Sweet Spot

Chapter 9. Customer Service in the Digital Age: Excellence in Every Interaction

Chapter 10: Strategies for Growth: Scaling Your Virtual Restaurant

Chapter 11: Future of Virtual Restaurants: Trends to Watch Out for

Chapter 12: Conclusion: The Recipe for Your DoorDash Success

Chapter 1: Introduction - The Dawn of Virtual Restaurant Business

In the heart of the 21st century, the way we do business is changing dramatically, and the restaurant industry is no exception. The advent of technology, combined with shifting consumer habits, has birthed a new era of dining: the age of virtual restaurants. This book will be your comprehensive guide to navigating and succeeding in this burgeoning landscape.

Virtual restaurants, also known as ghost kitchens or cloud kitchens, are restaurant concepts designed for delivery only, without a traditional dine-in space. These operations, stripped down to the kitchen and the digital interface, take orders via online platforms, with food delivered directly to the customer's doorstep. As technology continues to evolve, so too does the virtual restaurant concept, offering exciting new possibilities for restaurant entrepreneurs.

This guide will take you on a journey through the world of virtual restaurants on DoorDash, one of the leading food delivery platforms in the United States and globally. We'll explore the ins and outs of the business, from initial planning and startup, to operations, customer service, marketing, growth strategies, and beyond.

Our world has seen an unprecedented shift towards digital commerce, particularly emphasized by recent global events such as the COVID-19 pandemic. Homebound consumers have grown accustomed to the convenience of home delivery for all manner of goods and services. This shift has led to an exponential rise in the demand for home food delivery, placing the virtual restaurant business in an advantageous position.

While the digital space offers a vast pool of potential customers, it also brings with it its own set of challenges. The competition is fierce, and the online customer is discerning. To succeed in this industry, it's crucial to understand the platform, the market, the customers, and the strategies that can propel a virtual restaurant to success.

Throughout this book, we will delve into each aspect of running a successful virtual restaurant on DoorDash. We'll provide actionable insights, expert tips, and practical strategies to help you build a thriving business. We'll walk you through the essential steps and considerations to make your venture successful, whether you are a budding restaurateur venturing into the virtual space for the first time, an established restaurant owner looking to expand your online presence, or an entrepreneur seeking innovative ways to enter the food industry.

This is an exciting journey, and we are thrilled to be your guide. Welcome to the dawn of the virtual restaurant business, where culinary dreams meet digital innovation.

Remember, the business of food isn't just about delivering sustenance; it's about delivering experiences. It's about making people feel good about their choices, making them feel connected despite physical distances, and making them look forward to their next meal. So, let's begin this journey together and embrace the future of the food industry.

Chapter 2: Understanding DoorDash - A Comprehensive Guide

In this world of digital business, various online platforms offer their services to connect businesses and customers. Yet, among the plethora of choices, one platform stands out—DoorDash. Known for its efficiency and wide reach, DoorDash has quickly become an industry leader in food delivery services. This chapter will provide you with a comprehensive understanding of DoorDash, preparing you for your venture into the virtual restaurant business.

2.1 The Birth and Growth of DoorDash

DoorDash was born from a simple mission: to enable every merchant to deliver. The idea originated from a group of Stanford students who saw how businesses in their local area struggled to offer efficient delivery services. Launched in 2013 in Palo Alto, California, DoorDash started with just a handful of restaurants. The platform quickly gained popularity due to its efficiency, leading to rapid expansion. Today, DoorDash operates in over 4,000 cities across the U.S., Canada, and Australia, partnering with hundreds of thousands of businesses. Their expansive reach allows virtual restaurants to reach a broad customer base, fostering potential for substantial growth.

2.2 How DoorDash Works

To effectively use DoorDash as a platform for your virtual restaurant, it's crucial to understand its mechanics from both a customer and a restaurant partner perspective. Let's delve into the finer details of how DoorDash works.

Customer Perspective

For customers, the journey begins with either the DoorDash app or website. Upon opening the app or website, customers are presented with a selection of restaurants available in their area. They can search for specific restaurants, cuisines, or dishes, or browse through categories like "Fastest Near You," "Vegetarian," "DoorDash Deals," and more.

After selecting a restaurant, the customer is taken to the restaurant's menu page. Here, they can view the dishes on offer, along with prices and descriptions. Once they've chosen their items, they add them to their cart and proceed to checkout. Here, they can review their order, choose the delivery location, select a payment method, and finally place the order.

Once the order is placed, the customer can track the progress of their order in real-time— from the restaurant preparing the food, to when the Dasher picks it up, and finally, the delivery to their doorstep.

Restaurant Partner Perspective

As a restaurant partner, your journey begins with your business's listing on the DoorDash platform. Once a customer places an order from your restaurant, you'll receive a notification on your partnered device, usually a tablet provided by DoorDash. This device displays the order details, including the items ordered, any special instructions from the customer, and the delivery address.

Your responsibility is to prepare the order in a timely manner, ensuring the quality and accuracy of the food. Once the order is ready, you'll package it and mark it as ready for pick up in the DoorDash system.

At this point, DoorDash's system identifies and notifies a nearby Dasher to pick up the order. The Dasher then comes to your location, picks up the order, and delivers it to the customer. It's essential to have the order ready when the Dasher arrives to ensure a smooth pickup process and timely delivery.

Pairing Restaurants with Dashers

DoorDash uses an algorithm to efficiently pair Dashers with orders. The system considers factors like the Dasher's location, the delivery destination, current traffic conditions, and the estimated time it will take the restaurant to prepare the order. This sophisticated system is designed to optimize delivery times and ensure a seamless experience for both customers and restaurant partners.

Customer Service Issues

Sometimes, issues can arise in the process— perhaps a customer is unhappy with their order, or there's a delay in delivery. In such cases, DoorDash provides a customer service team to handle complaints and resolve issues. As a restaurant partner, you may be contacted by DoorDash's support team to address any issues related to the food quality or preparation. It's important to be responsive and cooperative in these situations to maintain your restaurant's reputation and ensure customer satisfaction.

Understanding this operational flow in detail will help you navigate the DoorDash platform efficiently, paving the way for a successful virtual restaurant business.

2.3 Becoming a DoorDash Partner

To kickstart your virtual restaurant journey, you'll first need to become a partner with DoorDash. The process is straightforward, but it involves a series of important steps. Let's take a deep dive into the process.

Preparation

Before you start the sign-up process, gather necessary information about your business. This includes your business name, address, contact details, operating hours, and a digital copy of your menu. In addition, you'll need to provide valid documents such as a business license and a food handler's permit.

Signing Up

Once you've gathered all the necessary details, visit the DoorDash Merchant Portal to initiate the signup process. Here, you'll be asked to fill in information about your restaurant, such as its location, operating hours, and menu. DoorDash will also require you to agree to their terms of service and fill out the necessary legal paperwork, including providing your bank information for receiving payments.

Onboarding Process

After your application is submitted, DoorDash will review it. If everything is in order, your partnership is approved, and the onboarding process begins. During this phase, you'll receive a welcome kit, typically containing a tablet for receiving orders, a DoorDash window decal, and other promotional materials.

DoorDash also provides training resources to help you and your team understand how to use the platform, manage orders, handle customer service issues, and optimize your listing.

Menu Setup

Setting up your menu on DoorDash is a crucial part of the process. You'll need to upload your menu items to the platform and add descriptions and prices. You can also add photos of your dishes, which can greatly enhance the appeal of your listing.

Take time to ensure your menu is set up correctly, as this will be the primary way customers engage with your restaurant. Make sure all descriptions are clear and appealing, prices are accurate, and the photos are high-quality and representative of the dish.

Launch

Once the setup is complete, your restaurant goes live on DoorDash, and customers can start placing orders. From this point, it's your responsibility to manage orders, ensure quality food preparation, and maintain timely preparation for pick-up by Dashers.

Commission Fees

Do note that DoorDash charges a commission on each order placed through the platform. This commission rate can vary and will be agreed upon during your sign-up process. It's essential to factor this into your pricing strategy and budget calculations.

Becoming a DoorDash partner provides your virtual restaurant with a broad customer base and a reliable delivery system, allowing you to focus on providing excellent food and service. As you go through this process, remember to be thorough and diligent, ensuring your restaurant is presented in the best possible light and is fully prepared for the exciting journey ahead.

2.4 DoorDash's Support for Virtual Restaurants

DoorDash is more than just a delivery platform; it's a partner that offers various resources and services to support the growth of your virtual restaurant. Let's delve into the details of the support services provided by DoorDash.

DoorDash Kitchens

DoorDash Kitchens is an innovative program offering shared kitchen spaces in selected locations. It's an ideal solution for virtual restaurants that need a professional kitchen setup without the hefty cost of owning or leasing a commercial kitchen. As a partner, you can prepare your food in these spaces, which are fully equipped with professional-grade appliances. This helps you save on overhead costs while maintaining the ability to cater to a high volume of orders.

Operational Support

DoorDash provides operational support to all its partners. As a partner, you get access to a comprehensive onboarding process and ongoing support to help you effectively run your business on the platform. This includes training on how to use the DoorDash Merchant Portal, managing and tracking orders, dealing with customer service issues, and using DoorDash's analytics tools.

Additionally, DoorDash's support team is available to help you with any issues or queries you might have about using the platform. Whether you're experiencing technical difficulties or have questions about a specific feature, DoorDash's support team is there to assist.

Marketing and Promotion

DoorDash helps increase the visibility of your virtual restaurant through various marketing initiatives. Your restaurant gets featured on the DoorDash app and website, and you can participate in promotional programs that can help attract more customers.

For example, you could be part of DoorDash Deals, which offers discounts to customers and encourages them to try out different restaurants. Also, your virtual restaurant could be highlighted in category sections like "New on DoorDash," "Local favorites," and others. This exposure can significantly boost your restaurant's visibility, helping to increase order volumes.

Business Analytics

One of the powerful tools you have access to as a DoorDash partner is the platform's comprehensive analytics. These analytics provide insights into your restaurant's performance, customer behavior, and sales trends. With this information, you can make data-driven decisions to optimize your menu, adjust your operating hours, or implement promotional activities.

In essence, DoorDash provides a well-rounded support ecosystem for virtual restaurants. It not only takes care of delivery logistics but also helps with operational, marketing, and strategic aspects of running a virtual restaurant. This support can be instrumental in the growth and success of your business on the platform.

2.5 Understanding the DoorDash User Interface

Navigating the DoorDash user interface effectively is crucial for running a successful virtual restaurant. Let's delve into the main components of the DoorDash interface, both on the merchant and customer side, and how to make the most of them.

Merchant Interface

As a DoorDash partner, you will interact with the DoorDash Merchant Portal, a dedicated interface where you can manage your restaurant's listing, track orders, and access business analytics. Here's a detailed breakdown:

* **Orders:** This tab displays incoming orders in real-time. You'll see the customer's order details, including the items ordered, any special instructions, and the expected pick-up time. Once an order is ready for pickup, you'll mark it as ready in this tab.

* **Menu:** In this section, you can add, edit, and remove menu items. Each item can be customized with a description, price, and photo. Special options and add-ons can also be added. It's essential to keep this section up-to-date and accurate to prevent customer confusion and dissatisfaction.

* **Business Information:** This section contains your restaurant's operating hours, contact details, and delivery zone. Any changes to your business operations, such as changes in hours or contact details, should be updated here promptly.

* **Ratings & Reviews:** Here, you'll see customer feedback on your restaurant and your food. Paying attention to these reviews and ratings can provide valuable insights into what you're doing well and areas where you could improve.

* **Analytics:** The analytics tab provides detailed information about your restaurant's performance, including sales data, popular dishes, peak order times, and customer demographics. Regularly reviewing these insights can guide you in making informed decisions to enhance your restaurant's performance.

Customer Interface

Understanding the customer interface is equally important, as this is how customers interact with your restaurant on DoorDash. Here are the key elements:

* **Restaurant Listing:** This includes your restaurant name, cuisine type, delivery time estimate, and customer rating. This is often the first impression customers get of your restaurant, so it's important to ensure that all the information here accurately represents your business.

* **Menu:** Customers browse your menu to decide what to order. This includes photos, descriptions, and prices of your dishes. High-quality photos and enticing descriptions can significantly influence customers' decisions.

* **Reviews and Ratings:** These are customers' assessments of your restaurant and your food. Potential customers often look at these when deciding whether to order from your restaurant. High ratings and positive reviews can greatly enhance your appeal.

* **Checkout and Payment:** Here, customers review their order, select a delivery address, choose a payment method, and place the order. The process is designed to be seamless and straightforward, ensuring a smooth ordering experience for customers.

Understanding the DoorDash user interface in its entirety enables you to effectively manage your virtual restaurant, maintain a positive relationship with your customers, and ultimately, optimize your success on the platform.

2.6 Navigating DoorDash Analytics

In the age of data-driven decisions, understanding and using the analytics provided by DoorDash can be a game-changer for your virtual restaurant. DoorDash Analytics is a suite of tools available in the Merchant Portal that provides valuable insights into your business's performance. Here's a breakdown of the various components and how you can utilize them effectively:

Sales Data

This section gives you an overview of your sales performance. You can view your total sales, average order value, and the number of orders over different time frames, such as daily, weekly, or monthly. This data can help you identify trends in your sales, helping you to understand your busiest periods and when sales might dip.

With this information, you can make strategic decisions, like running promotions during slower periods to boost sales or scheduling more staff during peak times to handle increased demand.

Popular Items

This feature shows you which items on your menu are selling the most. Knowing your top-selling items can guide menu planning, inventory management, and marketing efforts. For example, you could consider promoting these popular items further, bundling them with less popular items, or ensuring that they are always available to keep customer satisfaction high.

Customer Insights

DoorDash analytics also provides valuable information about your customers, such as their location, order frequency, and preferred delivery times. Understanding your customer demographics can help tailor your offerings and marketing strategies. For instance, if you find that most of your customers are ordering late at night, you might consider extending your operating hours or offering late-night specials.

Ratings and Reviews

This tool collects all the ratings and reviews left by customers. Monitoring this feedback can give you insights into what customers enjoy about your restaurant and areas where improvement may be needed. Positive feedback can be used in marketing materials (with the customers' consent), while constructive criticism can guide adjustments to your food or service.

Delivery Metrics

Here, you'll find information about delivery times, Dasher ratings for pick-ups at your restaurant, and customer feedback on delivery. This data can help identify any issues with the delivery aspect of your service, such as consistently long delivery times or problems reported by Dashers, allowing you to address these issues and improve your overall service.

Order Heatmap

This is a visual tool that shows the geographical distribution of your orders. A heatmap can help you understand where your customers are concentrated, informing decisions about possible expansion, marketing efforts, and delivery logistics.

To fully utilize DoorDash analytics, it's essential to regularly check these metrics and trends, continually optimizing your operations based on the insights gathered. The power of these analytics lies in their ability to provide a clear picture of your business's performance, enabling you to make informed decisions to grow and succeed as a virtual restaurant on the DoorDash platform.

Chapter 3: Building Your Virtual Restaurant: Startup Essentials

Running a successful virtual restaurant involves more than just signing up with DoorDash and setting up a menu. It's about creating an engaging brand, crafting a compelling menu, investing in the right technology, and, above all, delivering a consistent, high-quality food experience. Let's delve into the startup essentials for building your virtual restaurant.

3.1 Concept and Branding

The first step in launching your virtual restaurant is developing a unique and engaging concept. Your concept is the foundation of your brand; it communicates what you stand for, what kind of food you offer, and what makes you stand out in the crowded virtual restaurant space.

When defining your concept, consider factors such as your target audience, cuisine type, price point, and your unique selling proposition. Once your concept is defined, it should guide all other aspects of your business, from your menu to your marketing strategies.

Next, develop a compelling brand identity. This includes your restaurant name, logo, color scheme, and overall aesthetic. Your brand identity should reflect your concept and resonate with your target audience. It should also be consistent across all customer touchpoints, from your DoorDash listing to your packaging.

3.2 Menu Development

Your menu is one of your main tools for attracting and retaining customers. It should align with your concept, meet your customers' expectations, and stand out from the competition.

When developing your menu, consider the taste, presentation, pricing, and packaging of your dishes. Ensure that you have a mix of popular favorites and unique offerings that reflect your brand. Also, consider logistical factors, such as how well each dish will transport and how long it will retain its quality.

Once your menu is developed, present it effectively on your DoorDash listing. Use high-quality photos, compelling descriptions, and clear pricing. Also, consider implementing a dynamic menu strategy, adjusting your offerings based on customer feedback, sales data, and market trends.

3.3 Kitchen Setup and Operations

Efficient kitchen operations are crucial for a successful virtual restaurant. You need a kitchen setup that enables you to prepare high-quality food consistently and quickly. This may involve investing in professional-grade kitchen equipment, implementing effective food prep systems, and maintaining high standards of food safety and hygiene.

Consider how you'll fulfill DoorDash orders while potentially serving other channels. This may involve setting up a dedicated prep station and tablet for DoorDash orders.

Your operational efficiency also depends heavily on your team. Hire staff with the right skills and attitude, provide thorough training, and foster a positive, high-energy work environment.

3.4 Technology Investments

Investing in the right technology can streamline your operations and enhance your customer experience. This includes a reliable POS system, effective order management software, and possibly a kitchen display system.

Ensure that your tech setup integrates smoothly with the DoorDash platform, allowing you to receive orders seamlessly and manage your DoorDash operations effectively.

3.5 Customer Experience

Despite operating virtually, providing a great customer experience is just as important. This involves ensuring a smooth ordering process, delivering high-quality food, and resolving any issues promptly and professionally.

Pay close attention to your DoorDash reviews and ratings, and use this feedback to continuously improve your offerings and service. Remember, in the virtual restaurant business, customer satisfaction is key to repeat business and positive word-of-mouth.

3.6 Legal Considerations

Ensure that your virtual restaurant complies with all relevant regulations. This includes obtaining necessary permits and licenses, following food safety regulations, and complying with employment laws.

In addition, review the DoorDash partner agreement thoroughly and ensure that you understand and are comfortable with its terms.

Building a successful virtual restaurant involves careful planning, strategic decisions, and consistent execution. By focusing on these startup essentials, you can set your

virtual restaurant up for success from the outset and position yourself for growth and profitability in the booming virtual restaurant industry.

Chapter 4: Navigating The DoorDash Platform: A Detailed Walkthrough

Successfully operating a virtual restaurant on DoorDash requires more than just a great concept and delicious food; it requires a deep understanding of how the platform works, from setting up your restaurant and managing orders to resolving issues and using analytics. In this chapter, we will walk you through the ins and outs of the DoorDash platform.

4.1 Setting Up Your Restaurant

The process of setting up your virtual restaurant on DoorDash involves several key steps, each requiring thoughtful consideration and execution to help your business stand out in a competitive marketplace. In this section, we will guide you through each of these steps.

Restaurant Information

The first aspect of setting up your restaurant on DoorDash is inputting your business information. This includes:

* **Restaurant Name**: Choose a name that aligns with your brand and stands out to potential customers. Ensure it is easy to pronounce, remember, and search for.

* **Address**: The location of your kitchen should be accurately inputted. This is crucial because it determines your delivery radius.

* **Operating Hours**: You will need to specify your hours of operation. Consider peak meal times and the habits of your target market when determining these hours. Remember, you can always adjust your operating hours as you learn more about your customer demand patterns.

* **Contact Details:** Provide a valid contact number and email address where you can be reached for customer inquiries or issues.

* **Delivery Radius and Fees:** Your delivery radius is determined based on your kitchen location. It's important to set a delivery radius that is feasible for your delivery personnel to maintain quality and timeliness.

Additionally, you may choose to set delivery fees. These could be flat rates or variable based on distance.

Setting Up Your Menu

The next step is to establish your menu on the platform. The menu is essentially your primary sales tool on DoorDash. Here's how to set it up effectively:

* **Menu Items**: Start by listing all of your dishes. It's advisable to start with a limited but diverse menu to manage your operations efficiently and gauge customer response. You can always expand your menu over time based on customer demand and feedback.

* **Descriptions**: Write enticing yet honest descriptions for each dish. Clearly mention the ingredients, cooking method, and any other information that customers might find useful. Remember, your customers can't smell or taste your food through the app – your descriptions need to do that for them.

* **Pricing:** Ensure that your pricing is competitive yet profitable. Consider the costs of ingredients, preparation, packaging, and delivery when pricing your dishes.

* **Photos**: High-quality, appetizing photos are crucial for selling food online. Invest in professional food photography, if possible, or learn how to take great food photos yourself. For each dish, upload a well-lit, close-up image that showcases the dish's details and textures.

* **Customization Options and Add-Ons**: If you allow for customizations – such as no onions, extra cheese, or sauce on the side – make sure these options are clearly stated. Also, consider offering add-ons that complement your dishes and can increase your average order value, like a special dip with fries or a recommended drink with a meal.

* **Updates:** Regularly review your menu and update it based on performance, customer feedback, and market trends. Keep your menu fresh and engaging by adding new dishes, running specials, or featuring seasonal ingredients.

By carefully setting up your restaurant information and menu on DoorDash, you'll make a strong first impression on potential customers and set a solid foundation for your virtual restaurant business.

4.2 Managing Orders

Order management is a key component of your operations on DoorDash. This process encompasses several steps, from receiving and accepting an order to preparing it and having it picked up by a Dasher. In this section, we will provide a detailed overview of each step in the order management process.

Receiving Orders

Orders placed by customers on DoorDash will be instantly transmitted to you via the DoorDash Merchant Portal. Each incoming order triggers a notification, which can be set to an audible alert, making it hard to miss. These notifications will detail new orders requiring your attention.

The order ticket contains critical information, including:

* **Order Details:** This includes what items the customer has ordered, the quantity of each item, any customization or special requests, and the total price of the order.

* **Customer Information:** The ticket will also provide the customer's name, contact details, and delivery address. This is crucial information for the Dasher.

* **Special Instructions:** Some orders may come with special instructions from the customer. This can include requests for contactless delivery, additional condiments, or specific preparation instructions.

Accepting Orders

After reviewing the order details, the next step is to accept the order. Accepting the order promptly is crucial to maintaining a strong performance rating on DoorDash. This is because DoorDash tracks and rewards restaurants for maintaining high order acceptance rates and fast preparation times.

Once the order is accepted, the preparation time starts. This is the window within which you're expected to have the order prepared and ready for pickup. It's essential to adhere to this timeline to ensure customer satisfaction and maintain a strong partnership with DoorDash.

Preparing and Packaging Orders

Following order acceptance, your kitchen team should promptly begin preparing the order. Emphasis should be placed on consistency, ensuring that each dish aligns with its menu description and maintains the quality your brand promises.

While your food's taste is of utmost importance, the manner in which it's packaged can also significantly impact the customer's overall experience. Consider investing in high-quality, sturdy, and environmentally friendly packaging. Ensure that the packaging is appropriate for each type of dish, and that it helps to maintain the food's temperature and presentation during delivery.

Marking Orders as Ready for Pickup

As soon as an order is prepared, packaged, and ready to go, it should be marked as ready for pickup in the DoorDash Merchant Portal. This notification informs the Dasher that they can come to pick up the order.

Ensure that the order is correctly marked and is handed to the correct Dasher, cross-verifying with the name or order number provided by the Dasher. Remember, your interaction with the Dasher can impact how your restaurant is perceived and rated on the platform, so ensure it is a positive one.

Effective order management is crucial for operating a successful virtual restaurant on DoorDash. By understanding and mastering this process, you can ensure a smooth experience for your customers, Dashers, and your kitchen team alike.

4.3 Working with Dashers

Dashers, DoorDash's dedicated delivery personnel, are an essential part of the delivery ecosystem. They bridge the gap between your restaurant and your customers, physically delivering your dishes from your kitchen to your customers' tables. In this section, we will delve deeper into the integral role Dashers play, and provide guidelines for fostering a harmonious and efficient working relationship with them.

Understanding the Role of Dashers

Dashers use the DoorDash app to receive order pickup requests from restaurants. Once they accept a request, they proceed to the restaurant to pick up the order, then deliver it to the specified customer address.

From your restaurant's perspective, Dashers serve as your brand ambassadors in the field. They are often the only physical point of contact your customers have with your restaurant, and their conduct and professionalism can greatly influence your customers' experience.

Preparing for Dasher Arrival

Ensuring that your orders are ready for pickup by the specified time is crucial in maintaining a good working relationship with Dashers. If orders are regularly delayed, Dashers may become less inclined to accept pickup requests from your restaurant, which could ultimately affect your delivery times and customer satisfaction.

It's advisable to have a dedicated space in your restaurant for DoorDash orders, where Dashers can quickly and easily pick up orders without disturbing your restaurant's operations. Consider implementing a system for organizing orders so that Dashers can immediately identify the orders they are there to pick up.

Communicating with Dashers

Clear communication with Dashers can significantly streamline the pickup and delivery process. When Dashers arrive, ensure they know which order they are picking up and give them any necessary instructions or information about the order.

If a Dasher is late for a pickup, you can use the DoorDash Merchant Portal to notify DoorDash support. DoorDash will then contact the Dasher to ascertain the cause of the delay and provide you with updates.

Resolving Issues with Dashers

Occasionally, you may encounter issues with a Dasher, such as a Dasher failing to show up for a pickup or behaving unprofessionally. In such cases, you can report the issue to DoorDash through the Merchant Portal. DoorDash takes such reports seriously and will take appropriate action based on the nature of the issue.

Rating Dashers

At the end of each delivery, you will have the opportunity to rate the Dasher. Your ratings help DoorDash ensure a high standard of service by recognizing excellent Dashers and identifying those who may need additional support or training.

Dashers are integral to your restaurant's operations on DoorDash. By understanding their role and maintaining clear communication and professional interactions, you can help ensure smooth and efficient deliveries, leading to higher customer satisfaction and repeat business.

4.4 Resolving Issues and Providing Customer Service

Despite the best efforts, mishaps occur in the restaurant business. Whether it's an order mix-up, a customer complaint, or a technical issue, knowing how to respond effectively is crucial for maintaining customer satisfaction and your restaurant's reputation. In this section, we will explore how to handle such issues and deliver excellent customer service in the context of DoorDash.

Dealing with Common Issues

Here are a few common issues you might encounter and the suggested methods to handle them:

* **Order Mix-Ups:** If you or your staff realize an order has been mixed up, take immediate action. If the Dasher is still at your restaurant, correct the order before it leaves. If the order has already been dispatched, contact DoorDash support immediately. They can help coordinate with the Dasher and the customer to correct the issue.

* **Customer Complaints:** Complaints might range from food quality issues to delivery delays. In each case, listen to the customer's concerns,

apologize sincerely, and offer a resolution, such as a refund or credit towards a future order. Inform DoorDash support about the issue and your proposed resolution.

* **Technical Glitches:** If you experience issues with the DoorDash Merchant Portal, such as difficulties accepting orders or updating your menu, reach out to DoorDash support. They can assist you in troubleshooting the issue or escalate it to their technical team, if necessary.

Leveraging DoorDash Support

DoorDash provides support to its restaurant partners to assist with a range of issues. This includes help with order issues, customer complaints, Dasher-related problems, and technical glitches. You can reach DoorDash support via the Merchant Portal, and they can guide you through resolving issues or facilitate communication with Dashers or customers as needed.

Managing Reviews and Ratings

One of the most visible reflections of your restaurant's performance on DoorDash are your reviews and ratings. Customers rely heavily on these when choosing where to order from, making them a crucial aspect of your online reputation.

* **Monitoring Reviews:** Regularly check your reviews to understand what customers are saying about your food, delivery, packaging, and overall service. Negative reviews can offer insights into where you need to improve, while positive reviews can highlight what you're doing right.

* **Responding to Reviews:** Responding to reviews, both positive and negative, demonstrates that you value customer feedback. Thank the customers for positive reviews and assure unhappy customers that their

concerns are being addressed. Remember, your responses are public, so always maintain a respectful and professional tone.

* **Using Feedback for Improvement:** Use the feedback from your reviews to identify recurring issues and areas for improvement. Implement changes to address these issues, and consider letting your customers know that you've made these changes based on their feedback.

By effectively managing issues and providing excellent customer service, you can maintain a positive relationship with your customers, even when things go wrong. This can lead to increased customer loyalty, improved reviews, and ultimately, the success of your virtual restaurant on DoorDash.

4.5 Using Analytics

The DoorDash platform provides robust analytical tools that offer a wealth of information to help you run your virtual restaurant successfully. By understanding and leveraging these analytics, you can make data-driven decisions that can significantly enhance your business performance. In this section, we'll delve deeper into the types of analytics available and how you can use them effectively.

Understanding DoorDash Analytics

DoorDash provides a comprehensive suite of analytics across several critical business dimensions:

* **Sales Data:** This covers your total sales, average order value, number of orders, and top-selling items. Sales data can be analyzed over different time periods, such as daily, weekly, or monthly, to identify trends and patterns.

* **Customer Insights:** These analytics give you information about your customers' behavior. This includes data on new versus returning customers, popular delivery times, and average customer ratings.

* **Delivery Metrics:** These figures cover the delivery side of your business, including average delivery time, on-time rate, and Dasher ratings.

* **Feedback Reports:** These reports compile customer reviews and ratings, allowing you to easily monitor customer feedback.

Utilizing Analytics for Business Decisions

Regular review and analysis of these metrics can provide actionable insights to guide various aspects of your business:

* **Menu Optimization:** Sales data can reveal your best-selling and least-selling items. If certain dishes are consistently underperforming, it may be time to reconsider their place on your menu. Similarly, recognizing your top sellers can help you highlight them in your marketing efforts or offer them as specials.

* **Operating Hours:** Customer insights can show you your peak ordering times. If there's high demand outside your current operating hours, you might consider expanding your hours to capture more business.

* **Delivery Efficiency:** Delivery metrics can highlight areas of improvement in your delivery process. If your average delivery time is higher than the platform average, for instance, you might need to streamline your food preparation or packaging process.

* **Customer Satisfaction:** Reviewing feedback reports can provide insights into your customers' satisfaction. Look for recurring themes in your reviews to identify areas where your restaurant is excelling or lagging.

* **Marketing Initiatives:** Analyzing customer behavior can also guide your marketing initiatives. For example, if you have many new customers but few repeat customers, you might launch a loyalty program or special offers to encourage repeat business.

Using analytics is about more than just monitoring your restaurant's performance. It's about gaining insights into your business and using those insights to make strategic decisions that enhance your customer satisfaction, streamline your operations, and ultimately, boost your bottom line. By mastering DoorDash's analytical tools, you can position your virtual restaurant for success in the competitive food delivery landscape.

4.6 Participating in DoorDash Programs

DoorDash offers an array of programs and promotions designed to boost the visibility of your restaurant and stimulate sales. Involvement in these programs not only helps draw new customers but can also help build loyalty among existing patrons. This section delves deeper into some of these beneficial programs, providing insights on how they can be harnessed effectively for your virtual restaurant's growth.

Understanding DoorDash Programs

Here's an overview of two key programs DoorDash offers:

* **DoorDash Deals:** This feature allows you to set up special promotions and discounts, which are then prominently showcased on the DoorDash app. This can help attract deal-seeking customers and stimulate higher order volumes. Deals can range from percentage discounts to buy-one-get-one-free offers or combo deals.

* **DashPass:** DashPass is a subscription program for customers, offering them free delivery and reduced service fees on orders from participating

restaurants. Restaurants that are part of the DashPass program often see increased order volumes from DashPass subscribers, as customers are incentivized to order from DashPass restaurants to make the most of their subscription.

Leveraging DoorDash Programs for Your Business

Participating in DoorDash's programs can bring considerable advantages:

* **Boosting Visibility:** Your restaurant can gain increased visibility by being highlighted in the Deals section or being listed as a DashPass restaurant. This can help your restaurant stand out in a crowded marketplace and attract more customers.

* **Increasing Sales:** Offering deals can stimulate increased sales volumes, as customers are often drawn to promotions and discounts. Furthermore, DashPass can result in higher order volumes from subscribers seeking to maximize their subscription benefits.

* **Building Customer Loyalty:** Customers who take advantage of your deals or who regularly order from your restaurant through DashPass are more likely to become repeat customers, fostering customer loyalty.

Selecting the Right Programs for Your Restaurant

Not every program will be a perfect fit for every restaurant. It's important to review these opportunities and consider those that align with your business model, target audience, and financial goals.

For example, if you have higher profit margins and want to attract deal-seeking customers, offering discounts through DoorDash Deals might be a good fit. On the other hand, if you're looking to increase order volumes and are able to handle increased demand, joining the DashPass program might be more beneficial.

Remember, participation in these programs should be monitored and evaluated regularly to ensure they're providing a return on investment. Use the DoorDash analytics to track the performance of your deals and the impact of DashPass on your sales.

Understanding and leveraging the DoorDash platform's features can significantly enhance your restaurant's performance. By utilizing these tools and programs effectively, you can optimize your operations, deliver an outstanding customer experience, and stimulate growth in the dynamic world of virtual restaurants.

Chapter 5. Developing Your Menu: Attracting Customers through Gastronomy

5.1 Understanding Your Target Market: Who are you cooking for?

Before diving into the culinary side of your virtual restaurant, it's critical to understand your target market. Essentially, you need to answer the question: who are you cooking for? An in-depth understanding of your target market will guide not only your menu development but also your marketing strategies and business decisions. In this section, we'll delve into how to identify and understand your target market.

Identifying Your Target Market

Your target market is the specific group of people you aim to attract to your virtual restaurant. Here are some key factors to consider:

* **Geographic Location:** Since you're working with DoorDash, your potential customers will be in the areas you choose to serve. Research

the demographics, eating habits, and preferences of people in these areas.

* **Demographics:** Consider the age, gender, income level, occupation, and other demographic characteristics of your potential customers. For instance, a virtual restaurant in a college town might target students and faculty, while one near a business district might focus on working professionals.

* **Lifestyle:** This involves understanding your potential customers' behaviors, interests, and opinions. For example, are they health-conscious, or do they prefer indulgent comfort food? Do they value convenience and speed, or do they prioritize gourmet dining experiences?

* **Food Trends:** Stay current with food trends in your target market. For example, is there a growing demand for vegan, gluten-free, or locally sourced food?

Understanding Your Target Market

Once you've identified your target market, delve deeper to understand their food preferences and behaviors. Here are some strategies:

* **Customer Surveys:** Conducting surveys can help you gather direct feedback from potential customers about their food preferences, dietary restrictions, favorite cuisines, and more.

* **Market Research:** Look at existing studies and reports about your target market's eating habits. This might include data from the U.S. Bureau of Labor Statistics, industry reports, and health studies.

* **Competitor Analysis:** Review the menus and reviews of successful restaurants in your area that target a similar market. What dishes are popular? What do customers say they like or dislike?

Applying Your Understanding

Use your understanding of your target market to inform your menu development:

* **Menu Variety:** Ensure your menu caters to the tastes and dietary needs of your target market. For example, if your target market is health-conscious, offer a variety of nutritious, low-calorie dishes.

* **Pricing:** Your pricing should align with the spending habits of your target market. If your target market is price-sensitive, consider offering value meals or affordable dishes.

* **Marketing:** Tailor your marketing messages to resonate with your target market. Highlight aspects of your menu that align with their values and interests.

Understanding your target market is the first step in developing a menu that attracts customers. By knowing who you're cooking for, you can create a menu that resonates with your customers' tastes, meets their needs, and ultimately, drives the success of your virtual restaurant.

5.2 Defining Your Cuisine: Establishing Your Gastronomic Identity

Your cuisine is much more than just the type of food you serve; it's a reflection of your virtual restaurant's identity and brand. The cuisine you offer sets expectations for potential customers and helps differentiate your restaurant in a crowded marketplace. This section will guide you through the process of defining your cuisine and establishing your gastronomic identity.

Exploring Your Options

Choosing your cuisine isn't a decision to take lightly. Here are a few factors to consider:

* **Market Demand:** Your cuisine should align with the preferences of your target market. If you've already conducted market research, you should have a sense of what types of cuisine are popular in your area.

* **Competitive Landscape:** Consider the availability of different cuisines in your area. If there's already a glut of pizza places, for example, opening another one might not be the best decision unless you have a unique offering.

* **Operational Considerations:** Some cuisines might be more challenging or costly to prepare and deliver than others. Think about the ingredients, equipment, and skills needed to execute your menu successfully.

* **Your Passion and Expertise:** If you or your team have a particular passion or expertise for a certain type of cuisine, this can be a significant advantage. It will not only enhance the quality of your dishes but also imbue your brand with authenticity.

Establishing Your Gastronomic Identity

Once you've chosen a cuisine, the next step is to shape your gastronomic identity:

* **Menu Concept:** Your menu should have a clear and cohesive concept that aligns with your cuisine. Whether it's authentic Mexican street food, healthy vegan bowls, or gourmet French pastries, ensure that your dishes fit together harmoniously and reinforce your chosen identity.

* **Signature Dishes:** Consider developing one or more signature dishes — unique offerings that customers can't get elsewhere. These dishes can showcase your culinary creativity, emphasize your commitment to quality, and become a major draw for customers.

* **Ingredient Quality:** The quality of your ingredients can greatly influence the perception of your cuisine. Whether you're sourcing locally grown produce, importing exotic spices, or using organic meats, make sure your ingredients reflect the quality and values of your brand.

* **Preparation Techniques:** The way you prepare your dishes can also contribute to your gastronomic identity. This might involve using traditional cooking methods, innovative culinary techniques, or a signature style of presentation.

Communicating Your Cuisine

The final step is to communicate your cuisine to your potential customers:

* **Menu Descriptions:** Use your menu descriptions to convey not just what's in each dish, but also its flavors, textures, and culinary inspirations. This can help customers envision and appreciate your cuisine.

* **Food Photography:** High-quality photos can showcase the appeal of your cuisine. Use visual cues such as vibrant colors, fresh ingredients, and artistic plating to make your dishes look as good as they taste.

* **Brand Messaging:** Incorporate your cuisine into your overall brand messaging. This might include your restaurant's name, logo, tagline, and any marketing materials.

Defining your cuisine is a crucial step in developing your menu and establishing your virtual restaurant's identity. By choosing a cuisine that resonates with your target market, creating a cohesive and enticing menu, and communicating your gastronomic identity effectively, you can attract customers and set your virtual restaurant apart.

5.3 Crafting a Balanced Menu: Variety, Balance, and Appeal

Crafting a menu is an art and a science. It's not merely a list of dishes; it's a reflection of your restaurant's brand and a tool for attracting customers and driving sales. A well-crafted menu balances variety, appeal, and operational efficiency while aligning with your target market's preferences. In this section, we'll guide you through the process of creating a balanced and enticing menu for your virtual restaurant.

Variety: A Menu for Every Palate

Having a range of options caters to a broader audience and keeps customers coming back to try different dishes. But variety doesn't necessarily mean having a lengthy menu. Instead, focus on offering a diverse selection of dishes that represent your cuisine and appeal to different tastes, preferences, and dietary needs. Here are some points to consider:

* **Appetizers, Main Dishes, and Desserts:** Provide options for each course to offer a complete dining experience. Include lighter options and more substantial dishes.

* **Dietary Preferences:** Consider including vegetarian, vegan, gluten-free, or dairy-free options if they align with your target market's preferences.

* **Price Points:** Offer dishes at various price points to cater to different budgets.

* **Signature Dishes:** Highlight your unique dishes that set your restaurant apart.

5.4 The Art of Dish Description: Making Food Sound as Good as It Tastes

The way you describe your dishes can significantly impact your customers' perceptions and their decision to order. A good dish description should be more than a list of ingredients; it should tell a story that engages the senses and evokes an appetizing image of the dish. In this section, we'll delve into the art of dish description and provide some tips for making your food sound as good as it tastes.

Engaging the Senses

A compelling dish description engages multiple senses, not just taste. Here are some ways to engage each sense:

* **Sight:** Use words that convey color, size, shape, and presentation. For example, "golden brown, crispy fried chicken" or "a towering stack of fluffy pancakes drizzled with amber maple syrup."

* **Smell:** Highlight aromatic ingredients or cooking techniques, like "garlic-infused olive oil" or "smoky barbecue sauce."

* **Taste:** Describe the flavors in the dish, from the primary tastes (sweet, salty, bitter, sour, and umami) to more complex flavors. You might mention "the tangy burst of fresh tomatoes" or "the rich, velvety sweetness of dark chocolate."

* **Touch:** Convey the texture and temperature of the dish, such as "creamy, chilled avocado gazpacho" or "tender, melt-in-your-mouth beef brisket."

* **Sound:** Although less common in food descriptions, sound can be a powerful sensory cue. You might refer to the "sizzle of a hot fajita platter" or the "crunch of fresh lettuce."

Telling a Story

Your dish descriptions can also tell a story about each dish's origins, ingredients, or preparation methods. This can make your dishes more memorable and appealing, especially to customers who value authenticity, quality, or culinary creativity.

* **Origins:** Mention the dish's cultural or geographical roots, such as "a traditional Tuscan pasta dish" or "classic New York-style cheesecake."

* **Ingredients:** Highlight high-quality, unique, or locally-sourced ingredients, like "organic, free-range chicken" or "wild-caught Atlantic salmon."

* **Preparation:** Describe the cooking techniques or processes used in the dish, from "slow-roasted to perfection" to "hand-tossed pizza dough."

Writing Tips

Here are some general writing tips for crafting engaging dish descriptions:

* **Keep it concise:** While detail is important, avoid overloading your descriptions with too much information. Aim for a balance between evocative and concise.

* **Use sensory words:** Sensory words, like "crispy," "juicy," "melting," or "fragrant," can make your descriptions more vivid and enticing.

* **Avoid jargon:** Unless your target market is made up of food connoisseurs, avoid using too many technical culinary terms that might confuse your customers.

Crafting compelling dish descriptions is an art form that can significantly enhance your menu's appeal. By engaging the senses, telling a story, and using evocative language, you can make your food sound as good as it tastes and entice your customers to order.

While variety caters to customer preferences, balance ensures operational efficiency. A well-balanced menu takes into account the cost, preparation time, and popularity of each dish to maximize profits and customer satisfaction. Here are some factors to consider:

* **Ingredient Utilization:** Optimize the use of ingredients across multiple dishes to reduce waste and lower costs.

* **Preparation Complexity:** Balance simpler dishes with more complex ones to manage kitchen workload and ensure prompt delivery.

* **Popularity:** Monitor sales data to understand which dishes are most popular. A balanced menu should include a mix of high-selling dishes and lower-selling ones that might appeal to niche preferences.

Appeal: Enticing Customers with Delicious Descriptions and Photos

Appeal is about making your dishes sound and look as enticing as they taste. Here's how:

* **Dish Descriptions:** Craft descriptions that highlight the flavors, ingredients, and culinary techniques of each dish. Use sensory words to engage customers' imaginations.

* **Food Photography:** High-quality photos can make your menu visually appetizing. Invest in professional food photography to showcase your dishes.

* **Menu Design:** The layout and design of your menu can impact customers' perceptions and choices. Highlight signature or high-profit dishes, and organize dishes in a way that's easy to navigate.

Crafting a balanced menu is a strategic process that requires careful thought and ongoing refinement. By balancing variety, operational efficiency, and customer appeal, you can create a menu that attracts customers, drives sales, and represents your virtual restaurant's brand and gastronomic identity.

5.5 Pricing Your Menu: Balancing Costs, Perceived Value, and Profitability

Determining the right price for each item on your menu is critical to your virtual restaurant's success. It requires a careful balance between covering your costs, providing perceived value to your customers, and ensuring profitability for your business. In this section, we'll discuss how to price your menu effectively using these factors as a guide.

Cost-Based Pricing

The first step in pricing your menu is to understand your costs. These include the direct costs of ingredients and preparation, as well as indirect costs like labor, utilities, delivery fees, packaging, and the commission to DoorDash.

* **Food Cost Percentage:** This is a common restaurant metric that refers to the cost of ingredients as a percentage of the selling price. For example, if a dish costs $3 in ingredients and is sold for $10, the food cost percentage is 30%. A typical food cost percentage is around 25-35%, but this can vary depending on the type of cuisine and restaurant.

* **Total Cost Percentage:** Besides food costs, consider other costs such as labor, utilities, packaging, and DoorDash commission. A common target for total cost percentage (including food cost) is around 60-70%.

Perceived Value Pricing

Perceived value refers to the customer's assessment of the dish's worth or value. It depends not only on the quantity and quality of the food but also on factors like the dish's uniqueness, the quality of the ingredients, the complexity of preparation, the reputation of your restaurant, and the prices of similar dishes at other restaurants.

* **Competitor Analysis:** Check the prices of similar dishes at other local restaurants or virtual kitchens. This can give you a ballpark figure for what customers might be willing to pay.

* **Differentiation:** If your dish has unique features that differentiate it from others (like a secret family recipe or organic, locally-sourced ingredients), you might be able to price it higher and still offer good perceived value.

Profitability

Ultimately, your prices need to ensure profitability for your business. After covering all your costs, you should aim for a profit margin that supports your financial goals.

* **Profit Margin:** This is the difference between the selling price and the total cost, as a percentage of the selling price. For example, if a dish is sold for $10 and the total cost is $6, the profit margin is 40%.

* **Break-Even Analysis:** Determine how many orders of each dish you need to sell to cover your fixed costs (like rent or salaries). This can help you set sales targets and evaluate the feasibility of your prices.

Remember, menu pricing is not a one-time task. Monitor your costs, sales, and customer feedback regularly, and be prepared to adjust your prices as needed. While it's important to maintain competitive and fair pricing, it's equally important to ensure that your pricing strategy supports your virtual restaurant's sustainability and growth.

5.6 Regularly Updating Your Menu: Staying Fresh and Relevant

The menu of your virtual restaurant is not a static document. It should be considered as a dynamic tool that can be regularly updated and revised to keep your business fresh, interesting, and relevant to your customers. This section explores why and how you should consider regularly updating your menu.

Why Update Your Menu Regularly?

1. Seasonality: Different ingredients are in peak season at different times of the year. By regularly updating your menu, you can take advantage of the freshest seasonal ingredients, which often have superior flavor and are more cost-effective.

2. Customer Preferences: Trends in food and dining evolve over time. By keeping your menu up to date, you can cater to changing customer preferences and demands. Moreover, regular customers will appreciate new dishes to try, keeping their dining experience exciting and engaging.

3. Operational Efficiencies: You might identify dishes that are not selling as well or are more time-consuming or costly to prepare. Regularly reviewing and updating your menu allows you to refine your offerings for better operational efficiency and profitability.

4. Marketing Opportunities: New menu items can be excellent marketing tools. They can create buzz and give you something new to promote on social media, newsletters, or on the DoorDash platform itself.

How to Update Your Menu Effectively?

1. Data-Driven Decisions: Use your DoorDash analytics to understand which dishes are your best sellers and which ones are underperforming. Look at customer reviews and feedback for insights into what's working and what's not.

2. Test New Dishes: Before making a permanent change to your menu, consider testing new dishes as specials. This allows you to gauge customer response and make necessary tweaks before fully committing to the change.

3. Communicate Changes: Whenever you update your menu, ensure you communicate these changes to your customers. Use your online platforms like social media or email newsletters to announce new dishes, and consider offering promotions to encourage customers to try them.

4. Train Your Staff: Make sure your kitchen and customer service staff are well-informed about any menu changes. They should understand how new dishes are prepared and be able to answer any questions customers might have.

5. Update Your DoorDash Listing: Finally, ensure your updated menu is accurately reflected on DoorDash. Include enticing photos and descriptions for any new dishes to attract customer interest.

Remember, the goal of regularly updating your menu is to improve your business — whether by increasing customer satisfaction, reducing costs, improving operational efficiency, or staying current with industry trends.

Keep your finger on the pulse of your business, listen to your customers, and don't be afraid to make changes for the better.

5.7 Promoting Your Menu on DoorDash: Highlighting Your Culinary Delights

Once you have crafted a compelling and appetizing menu, the next step is to ensure it reaches and attracts your target audience. DoorDash provides several opportunities to promote your menu to potential customers, helping to highlight your culinary delights and entice orders. In this section, we'll discuss some strategies for effectively promoting your menu on DoorDash.

1. Optimize Your Listing

The first place to focus your efforts is on your DoorDash listing itself. This is where customers will discover your virtual restaurant and browse your menu. Here are some ways to optimize your listing:

* **High-Quality Photos:** As we've discussed, enticing photos are a critical component of your menu. Make sure your listing features high-quality images of your dishes to catch the eye and stimulate the appetite.

* **Detailed Descriptions:** Accompany each photo with a detailed and enticing description. Use sensory language and highlight the unique features of each dish.

* **Easy Navigation:** Organize your menu into clear categories (like "Appetizers," "Main Dishes," "Desserts") to help customers easily navigate your offerings.

* **Highlight Specialties:** If you have dishes that are particularly popular or unique, consider featuring them prominently on your listing. You could also use labels like "Chef's Recommendation" or "Best Seller."

2. Participate in DoorDash Programs

DoorDash offers several programs and promotions that can help to increase your visibility and appeal on the platform. These include:

* **DoorDash Deals:** This feature allows you to offer special promotions or discounts, which can encourage customers to try your restaurant.

* **DashPass:** Participating in this subscription program can make your restaurant more appealing to DashPass subscribers, who receive benefits like reduced delivery fees.

* **Try Me Free:** New restaurants on DoorDash may be eligible for the "Try Me Free" promotion, which offers free delivery to customers to encourage them to try your restaurant.

3. Respond to Reviews

Customer reviews on DoorDash can significantly influence other customers' decisions. Regularly monitor your reviews and take the time to respond – thank customers for positive reviews, and address any issues raised in negative reviews. This shows that you value customer feedback and are committed to delivering a great dining experience.

4. Use Social Media

While not directly on the DoorDash platform, your social media channels can be an effective tool for promoting your menu. Regularly share photos and updates about your dishes, and encourage your followers to order through DoorDash.

By promoting your menu effectively on DoorDash, you can increase your virtual restaurant's visibility, attract more customers, and ultimately drive more orders. Always keep your target market in mind, and aim to create a listing that not only showcases your culinary delights but also communicates your restaurant's unique identity and values.

Chapter 6: Winning with Photography: How to Showcase Your Food

Visual appeal plays a critical role in food selection, particularly in the context of online ordering where customers can't smell or taste the dishes before deciding. High-quality, appetizing photographs can significantly enhance your menu's appeal and lead to more orders. This chapter provides detailed guidance on how to effectively showcase your food through photography.

6.1 The Importance of Food Photography

Food, as they say, is eaten first with the eyes. The sensory experience of dining begins not with the first bite, but with the first glimpse. This is especially true in the context of online food ordering, where the decision to purchase is heavily influenced by the visual representation of the menu. Therefore, high-quality food photography is not just an aesthetic choice but a crucial element in the success of your virtual restaurant. In this section, we delve into why food photography is so essential and how the right images can stimulate cravings, evoke sensory experiences, and influence purchasing decisions.

Visual Appetite Trigger

The primary role of food photography is to whet the appetite - to make viewers feel hungry and crave the dish. A well-crafted image can showcase the freshness and quality of ingredients, the textures, and even suggest the aroma of the dish. The aim is to evoke a visceral, almost Pavlovian response in the viewer, leading them to want to taste the dish.

Influencing Buying Decisions

When customers browse through a food delivery app like DoorDash, they make quick decisions based on the images they see. If a picture is enticing, it can significantly influence the customer's choice, even among countless options. A dish that looks appetizing and appealing is far more likely to be ordered than one that is poorly presented or lacking an image at all.

Building Your Brand

Your food photos are a reflection of your brand. They convey your restaurant's quality, attention to detail, and culinary style. Consistently high-quality images can help to build a strong, positive brand identity in customers' minds. This can lead to increased loyalty and repeat orders.

Sharing and Social Media Engagement

In the age of social media, people love to share images of food. Having stunning images of your dishes not only makes your menu more appealing but also increases the chances of customers sharing these images on their social media platforms. This serves as free marketing, potentially reaching a larger audience.

Trust and Transparency

Finally, good food photography shows transparency. It assures the customer that what they see is what they will get. It builds trust, an essential factor in the customer's decision to order from your restaurant.

In conclusion, investing in high-quality food photography is a vital aspect of running a successful virtual restaurant. It's not just about making food look good; it's about connecting with customers on a sensory and emotional level, influencing their buying decisions, enhancing your brand, and ultimately increasing your sales.

6.2 Basic Principles of Food Photography

Mastering the art of food photography requires a solid understanding of some fundamental principles. These principles, including composition, lighting, color balance, focus, and the artful use of props, are the bedrock upon which appealing and appetizing food photographs are built. Let's delve into each of these topics and see how they apply in food photography.

Composition

Composition refers to how elements are arranged within your frame. An effectively composed photograph is balanced, draws the viewer's eye to the main subject (your food), and tells a story.

In food photography, consider the placement of your dish, the angle you're shooting from, and how you're using space. Some dishes look best when shot from above (like pizzas or salads), while others benefit from a side angle (like burgers or layered cakes).

One crucial rule of composition is the "rule of thirds." Imagine dividing your image into nine equal squares (like tic-tac-toe). The points where these lines intersect are your points of interest. Placing your dish at these intersections can create a balanced, appealing image.

Lighting

Lighting is, arguably, the most crucial aspect of photography, and food photography is no exception. Good lighting brings out the vibrant colors of your food, enhances texture, and adds depth to your image.

Natural light is the gold standard for food photography. It's soft, diffused, and brings out the true colors of your food. If possible, shoot next to a window with indirect sunlight. Avoid using flash as it can create harsh shadows and highlights.

Color Balance

Color balance is all about ensuring the colors in your photograph are accurate. Improper white balance can give your photo a blue (cool) or yellow (warm) tint, which can make your food look unappetizing.

Most cameras and smartphones have a 'White Balance' setting. For most indoor, natural light situations, the 'Auto' or 'Daylight' setting works fine. If your images still have a color cast, this can be corrected during post-production.

Focus

Focus is key in food photography. Your main dish should be sharp and clear, drawing the viewer's attention. Using a shallow depth of field (where the main subject is in sharp focus and the background is blurred) can add a professional touch to your photos. This effect can be achieved using the 'Portrait' or 'Aperture Priority' mode on most cameras and smartphones.

Using Props

Props can enhance your food photos by adding context, creating a story, and filling empty space. They can be as simple as cutlery, napkins, ingredients, or a drink. Remember, though, the food is the star - props should complement, not distract. Stick to a color scheme that matches your food and brand style.

Texture and Details

Finally, capturing the texture and details of your dish can add depth and allure to your photo. The bubbling cheese on a pizza, the steam rising from a bowl of soup, or the glistening glaze on a donut can be very enticing. Don't be afraid to get close and capture these tantalizing details.

In summary, while food photography can seem complex, understanding these basic principles can significantly improve the quality of your images. With practice, you'll develop an eye for composition, lighting, and details, leading to more appealing and appetizing food photos.

6.3 Do-It-Yourself Tips for Food Photography

Budget constraints are a reality for many virtual restaurants, particularly those just starting out. However, that doesn't mean you can't create beautiful, enticing food photos on your own. With a little knowledge, practice, and creativity, you can capture high-quality images that do your dishes justice. Here are some practical tips to get you started.

Necessary Equipment

While professional photographers use high-end DSLR or mirrorless cameras, most modern smartphones have excellent cameras that are more than capable of capturing stunning food photos. Use a tripod to keep your shots steady, especially in low-light conditions. A simple reflector (even a piece of white cardboard can work) can be used to bounce light and soften shadows.

Setting Up a Home Studio

You don't need a professional studio to take great food photos. Any space with good natural light (like a table near a window) can serve as your makeshift studio. Use a neutral tablecloth or a wooden board as your base. Collect a variety of props like cutlery, plates, glasses, napkins, and even ingredients to add context and story to your photos.

Do's and Don'ts

Do:

1. Use natural light: It's the best light for food photography, and it's free.
2. Experiment with angles: Some dishes look better from above, while others look better from the side.
3. Pay attention to composition: Arrange your dish and props carefully to create balance and appeal.
4. Be patient: Great photos take time. Don't rush.

Don't:

1. Use flash: It creates harsh shadows and highlights.
2. Overcomplicate your shot: The food is the star. Keep it simple.
3. Ignore editing: Simple edits can enhance your photo. There are plenty of free editing apps available.
4. Forget to clean up: Clean the edges of your plates, remove crumbs, and wipe away any smears.

6.4 Working with a Professional Food Photographer

If your budget allows, hiring a professional food photographer can take your visual content to the next level. A professional will have the technical skills, experience, and equipment to capture your dishes in the best possible light. Here's how to make the most of this investment.

Selecting a Food Photographer

Start by reviewing the photographer's portfolio to ensure their style aligns with your brand. Look for experience with food photography specifically, as it's a unique discipline. Ask for recommendations from other restaurants or food industry contacts.

Preparing for the Shoot

Before the shoot, have a clear idea of what you want. Which dishes will you be shooting? Will you include props or ingredients? What kind of mood or style are you aiming for? Communicate these details to your photographer to ensure you're on the same page.

Consider hiring a food stylist for the shoot. They specialize in preparing food for the camera and can make your dishes look their best.

Making the Most of Your Investment

Once you've invested in professional photos, use them widely. They should feature prominently on your DoorDash menu, but also consider using them on your website, social media channels, and any other promotional materials. Regularly refresh your images to keep your content current and engaging.

Whether you're going the DIY route or hiring a professional, remember that great food photography is about more than just pretty pictures. It's a powerful marketing tool that can significantly enhance your virtual restaurant's appeal and success.

6.5 Editing and Post-Production

While capturing a great shot is the first step, post-production is where your food photography truly comes to life. Even the most basic editing can enhance your images and make them stand out. Here are some fundamental editing steps to elevate your food photos:

Cropping: Cropping helps eliminate unnecessary elements in the frame and draw attention to the main subject – your dish. Always maintain the rule of thirds when cropping your image. This simple compositional principle creates balance and draws the viewer's eye to the most engaging parts of the photo.

Adjusting Lighting and Colors: Adjusting exposure, contrast, and brightness can greatly enhance the overall mood of your photo. Increase brightness and contrast sparingly to make your image pop, but avoid overexposing it. You may also want to adjust the temperature, saturation, and vibrancy to make the colors of your food more appetizing.

Removing Distractions: Sometimes, there may be elements in the photo that distract the viewer from the main subject. Using editing tools, you can remove these distractions to focus on your dish. These might include crumbs, smudges, or any stray items that managed to sneak into your frame.

For post-production, there are numerous software options available, both paid and free, such as Adobe Lightroom, Snapseed, and VSCO. Take the time to familiarize yourself with these tools, as they can make a substantial difference in your food photography.

6.6 Best Practices for Displaying Photos on DoorDash

High-quality photos are an essential ingredient for success on DoorDash, but it's equally important to display them effectively. Here are some best practices for showcasing your photos on DoorDash:

Choosing a Cover Photo: The cover photo is the first image customers see when they visit your restaurant on DoorDash. It should be a strong, enticing image that represents your restaurant well. This could be a photo of your signature dish or a collage of several popular items.

Displaying Multiple Photos Per Dish: Customers appreciate seeing multiple angles and close-ups of a dish. If possible, include several photos for each item to give customers a comprehensive idea of what they're ordering.

Regularly Updating Your Photos: Just like updating your menu, updating your photos is a way to keep things fresh and engaging for customers. Regularly adding new photos can highlight seasonal dishes, specials, or new additions to your menu.

Remember, on a platform like DoorDash, your photos serve as the primary interaction customers have with your food. Therefore, showcasing appetizing, high-quality, and realistic photos of your dishes is not just recommended, but essential for your virtual restaurant's success. Following these guidelines will help attract customers, build trust, and ultimately, increase your sales.

Chapter 7. Food Preparation: Tips and Tricks for Efficiency and Quality*

In the world of food delivery, where every minute counts, efficiency in food preparation can make a significant difference. At the same time, it's crucial not to compromise the quality of your dishes. This chapter will provide practical advice on maintaining this balance in your virtual restaurant.

7.1 Streamlining Your Kitchen Operations

In the competitive landscape of food delivery, efficiency is the name of the game. A well-structured, streamlined kitchen operation is vital for maintaining a smooth workflow, reducing prep time, and delivering customer orders promptly. Here's how you can achieve that.

Designing a Functional Kitchen Layout

The kitchen layout is the backbone of your operation. It should facilitate smooth movement and easy access to kitchen equipment and ingredients. Aim for a layout that follows the natural flow of food preparation - from receiving and storing ingredients to preparation, cooking, plating, and finally, packing for delivery.

Consider a zone-based layout, with distinct areas for different activities. For example, have a dedicated area for raw ingredient prep (washing, peeling, cutting), a separate zone for cooking (stoves, ovens, grills), a plating station where dishes are assembled, and a packing area where orders are prepared for delivery. This minimizes cross-contamination and helps staff avoid getting in each other's way during busy periods.

Regular Equipment Maintenance

Regular maintenance and servicing of kitchen equipment are vital for preventing unexpected breakdowns that could disrupt your operations. Ensure your equipment is cleaned daily, and schedule regular check-ups for your ovens, refrigeration units, dishwashers, and any other appliances you frequently use. Regular servicing not only prolongs the lifespan of your equipment but also ensures they run at optimal efficiency.

Investing in Quality Equipment

Investing in high-quality, commercial-grade kitchen equipment can significantly speed up your cooking processes. For example, high-performance ovens can cook food more evenly and quickly than conventional models. High-capacity food processors can significantly reduce manual chopping time.

Remember, the right equipment is an investment, not an expense. While commercial-grade equipment may have higher upfront costs, they often result in long-term savings due to their durability and efficiency.

Organizing Ingredients and Supplies

A well-organized kitchen can drastically improve your efficiency. Consider implementing a standardized system for organizing your ingredients. Label storage containers and use a First-In-First-Out (FIFO) system to ensure ingredients are used before they expire.

Ingredients commonly used together in recipes should be stored close to each other. Store items at their appropriate temperatures to maintain freshness and prevent spoilage. Regularly review your organization system and adjust it as necessary based on what's working and what's not.

Implementing Standard Operating Procedures (SOPs)

Standard Operating Procedures, or SOPs, are documented processes that a restaurant must follow to ensure consistency and efficiency. They provide step-by-step instructions for routine tasks, from prepping ingredients to cleaning the fryers. Implementing SOPs can significantly improve your kitchen's efficiency and ensure that everyone knows their roles and responsibilities.

By streamlining your kitchen operations, you can ensure a smooth workflow, reduce errors and delays, and ultimately, increase your productivity and profitability.

7.2 The Art of Pre-Preparation

Mastering pre-preparation, known in the culinary world as mise-en-place, is an essential step to ensuring both efficiency and quality in your virtual restaurant. Rooted in French cuisine, mise-en-place is more than just a practical method; it's a philosophy that encourages mindfulness and orderliness in the kitchen.

First, let's discuss what mise-en-place encompasses. It means having all your ingredients ready before the cooking process begins. This could include cleaning and chopping vegetables, marinating meats, measuring out spices, or pre-cooking certain parts of your dishes. For instance, if you're preparing a complex dish like a lasagna, you might make your sauces ahead of time, grate your cheese, and pre-cook your noodles. Then, when it's time to assemble the lasagna, everything is at your fingertips.

This approach requires some initial investment of time, but the benefits it reaps are well worth it. Here are three key advantages of adopting the mise-en-place method:

Efficiency: By preparing everything beforehand, you significantly speed up the actual cooking process. Instead of pausing to chop an onion or measure out a spice, everything is ready to go. This is especially crucial during peak hours when orders are coming in fast, and you need to be as time-efficient as possible.

Stress reduction: A smooth cooking process can reduce stress in the kitchen. When everything is prepared and organized, you can focus solely on cooking, reducing the chance of errors, and minimizing the chaos that can often happen in busy kitchens.

Consistency: Ensuring consistency in your dishes is key to building a reliable brand. By measuring out ingredients in advance, you can ensure that each serving has the same quantity and taste. This meticulous approach can help maintain a consistent quality that customers can rely on.

Mise-en-place is a commitment to discipline and organization. In the fast-paced environment of a virtual kitchen, it can be your secret weapon for delivering quality dishes efficiently. Whether it's a gourmet burger or a delicate pastry, every meal you serve will carry the mark of thoughtful preparation that customers can taste and appreciate.

7.3 Quality Control in Food Preparation

Quality control in food preparation can make the difference between a thriving restaurant and one that quickly loses traction. With the virtual restaurant landscape growing more competitive by the day, maintaining a consistent, high-quality product offering is more crucial than ever. Below, we'll delve into some key strategies for ensuring optimal quality control in your kitchen.

Standard Recipes:

Creating standard recipes for each dish is a fundamental step for ensuring consistency. These recipes should include specific measurements for each ingredient, detailed preparation steps, cooking times, and presentation guidelines. Each recipe should be documented and accessible to every member of your kitchen staff to reference as needed.

Standard recipes are beneficial for several reasons. They eliminate guesswork in the kitchen, streamline the cooking process, and ensure a uniform output. This is particularly important when different chefs may be working on the same dish at different times. It ensures that every customer receives the same quality of food, regardless of when or who prepared it.

Staff Training and Monitoring:

Once you've established your standard recipes, it's essential to train your kitchen staff thoroughly. They should understand the importance of adhering to these standards and the impact it has on the customer experience. Ongoing training sessions can be helpful to reinforce these standards and introduce any new recipes.

Regular monitoring of the kitchen operations is also crucial. It allows you to observe the adherence to the standard recipes, rectify any deviations immediately, and recognize and address any issues with the cooking processes. Regular feedback can also help your staff improve and maintain their performance.

Hygiene and Food Safety:

Adhering to stringent hygiene and food safety standards is paramount in the food industry. It's not only a legal obligation but also a matter of protecting your customers' health and your restaurant's reputation. Ensure your staff understand and comply with all local health and safety regulations.

Your kitchen should be equipped with adequate facilities for hand washing and sanitizing tools and surfaces. Staff should be trained on proper food handling and storage techniques, like keeping raw and cooked foods separate, maintaining proper temperatures, and regularly checking the freshness of ingredients.

Maintaining high hygiene standards doesn't just protect you from potential health code violations or foodborne illness incidents; it can also impact the quality of your food. A clean and well-organized kitchen is more conducive to efficient, high-quality food preparation.

In conclusion, implementing quality control in your kitchen can significantly enhance your restaurant's operations and customer satisfaction. By maintaining consistent standards, training and monitoring your staff, and adhering to strict hygiene practices, you can provide a product that your customers trust and enjoy time and time again.

7.4 Batch Cooking and Portion Control

Managing a bustling virtual restaurant requires a unique blend of efficiency and precision. Among the strategies to consider are batch cooking and portion control, which can help streamline operations and maintain consistency in your offerings. Let's delve into how to effectively implement these methods in your kitchen.

Batch Cooking: Efficiency Meets Quality

Batch cooking involves preparing large quantities of a particular dish at one time. This method can be a significant time saver, allowing you to service more orders without the need to start the cooking process from scratch for each one. However, it's essential to balance this efficiency with a commitment to quality and freshness.

Proper storage is the cornerstone of successful batch cooking. Invest in high-quality, airtight storage containers to keep prepared dishes fresh. Remember to cool cooked food rapidly before storing it in the refrigerator or freezer to prevent the growth of harmful bacteria. Always label these containers with the contents and date of preparation to keep track of their freshness.

Avoid reheating the entire batch when fulfilling an order. Instead, portion out the needed amount and reheat only that, leaving the remaining amount chilled. This practice helps maintain the food's texture and taste and prevents the growth of bacteria that can occur from multiple reheating.

Portion Control: Consistency, Cost Management, and Waste Reduction

Alongside batch cooking, implementing portion control can play a crucial role in your kitchen. The goal of portion control is twofold. First, it ensures that each customer receives the same quantity of food, promoting consistency across your orders. Second, it helps manage food costs and minimize waste by ensuring that you're utilizing your ingredients optimally.

Start by establishing standard portion sizes for each dish on your menu. This could mean weighing a piece of meat, measuring a scoop of rice, or counting the number of ravioli per serving. Whatever the case, each serving should contain the same amount of food, and your kitchen staff should be trained accordingly.

Utilizing the right tools can aid in portion control. Scales, measuring cups, and portion scoops can be used to ensure that each serving is consistent. Similarly, using portion control containers for storing pre-portioned ingredients can streamline the cooking process.

By integrating batch cooking and portion control in your kitchen operations, you can deliver a consistent, quality product in an efficient manner. This approach not only enhances the customer experience but can also contribute to more predictable food costs and less waste. So, while it may require a bit of planning and training upfront, the payoff will be worth the effort.

7.5 Adapting Recipes for Delivery: The Art of Travel-Friendly Cuisine

Preparing food for a delivery-oriented business requires a different mindset compared to a traditional dine-in restaurant. While taste and presentation remain crucial, a new factor comes into play: how well the dish travels. As your food will spend some time in transit, you need to ensure that it arrives at your customers' doorsteps in the best possible condition.

Cooking Times and Techniques

The first factor to consider is cooking time. As a rule of thumb, it's prudent to slightly undercook items that continue to cook from residual heat and could potentially become overcooked during delivery. This applies especially to proteins like steak, fish, and chicken.

For dishes that include crispy or crunchy elements, consider cooking them to be a bit more well-done than usual. The additional moisture in the delivery packaging can sometimes soften these elements, so a slightly longer cooking time can help maintain their texture during transit.

Packaging Strategies

The way you pack your food can also make a big difference in how well it travels. Consider packing sauces and dressings separately to prevent dishes from becoming soggy. You could also think about compartmentalized packaging to keep different components of a dish separate, retaining the distinct flavors and textures.

Temperature also plays a significant role. Consider using insulated delivery bags to keep hot foods hot and cold foods cold during transportation. For items that need to be served cold like salads or desserts, consider instructing your customers to refrigerate them briefly upon delivery for the best experience.

Choosing the Right Ingredients

Finally, be mindful of the ingredients you use. Some ingredients may not hold up well during delivery. For example, delicate greens might wilt, and crispy items might lose their crunch. On the other hand, sturdy vegetables, grains, and proteins that retain their texture and flavor well over time can be excellent choices for delivery-friendly dishes.

Consider running tests with your menu items to see how they hold up after spending some time in a delivery container. This could involve packing a dish as if for delivery, leaving it for the typical delivery time, and then evaluating its taste and presentation.

Remember, your goal is to create a memorable dining experience, even if your customers are dining at home. Taking the time to adapt your recipes for delivery can ensure that your food arrives at its destination just as delicious as it would be served straight from your kitchen. With a little creativity and experimentation, you can master the art of travel-friendly cuisine and delight your customers with every order.

Chapter 8. Pricing Strategies for Success: Finding the Sweet Spot

Developing an effective pricing strategy is a critical aspect of running a successful virtual restaurant. Pricing your menu items correctly can influence customer behavior, impact your profitability, and determine your business's long-term viability. In this chapter, we will delve into different pricing strategies, factors influencing menu pricing, and tips on finding the right price points for your offerings.

8.1 Understanding Food Cost and Profit Margins

The cornerstone of any successful pricing strategy lies in a comprehensive understanding of your food costs and desired profit margins. This understanding is crucial because it not only allows you to cover the cost of ingredients but also to account for other operational costs and leave room for satisfactory profit margins.

Food Cost Calculation

Food cost refers to the cost of all the ingredients used to prepare a dish. This cost should take into account every single ingredient that goes into the dish, even seemingly insignificant ones like a pinch of salt or a dash of oil, as they can add up over time.

To calculate the food cost for a specific dish, you need to:

1. List all the ingredients used in the recipe.
2. Determine the cost of each ingredient. This cost is typically calculated by the cost per unit or cost per kilogram/liter, depending on the ingredient.
3. Calculate the amount of each ingredient used in the recipe and multiply this by the cost per unit to get the total cost of each ingredient.
4. Sum up the total costs of all ingredients. This will give you the total food cost for the dish.

For example, if you're making a pasta dish, you need to consider the cost of the pasta, the sauce, the meat or vegetables, and any spices or garnishes. Each ingredient's cost must be calculated based on the quantity used in that particular dish.

Profit Margins

Once you have your food cost, the next step is to determine your selling price that would ensure a satisfactory profit margin. Profit margin is the difference between the selling price and the total cost of the dish, expressed as a percentage of the selling price.

For example, if your food cost for a dish is $5 and you want a profit margin of 70%, your selling price would need to be around $16.67.

A general rule of thumb in the restaurant industry is to aim for a food cost percentage of around 30%, meaning that the cost of the ingredients should be about 30% of the selling price. However, this can vary depending on factors like the type of cuisine, the restaurant's location, and the target customer base.

Other Costs

It's important to remember that the selling price must also cover indirect costs such as utilities, labor, packaging, delivery charges, and more. These costs should be distributed across all your dishes, which might increase the selling price further.

Understanding your food costs and profit margins is the first step in setting your menu prices. A well-defined pricing strategy that covers all costs and provides a reasonable profit margin can set your virtual restaurant up for financial success. Keep in mind that these calculations are not a one-time task; they must be regularly reviewed and adjusted to reflect changes in ingredient costs, operational costs, and market conditions.

8.2 Competitor Analysis and Market Positioning

Setting the right prices involves a delicate balance between covering costs, securing profits, and offering value to your customers. But to strike that balance effectively, you need to understand the market in which you operate. This involves a careful analysis of your competitors and a clear understanding of your restaurant's market positioning.

Conducting a Competitor Analysis

To gauge the competitive landscape, start by identifying other restaurants in your area that serve similar types of cuisine or have a similar concept to yours. Check out their menus on the DoorDash platform, focusing on both their pricing and their offerings. Try to understand what sets them apart – it could be the type of ingredients they use, their portion sizes, their presentation style, or any additional services they provide.

Understand that it's not about mimicking their prices; instead, it's about understanding the existing market dynamics and what customers might expect to pay for a particular type of food or dining experience.

For instance, if you're a pizza place and all the other pizza places in your area charge between $10 to $15 for a pizza, you should consider whether charging $20 would make sense to your customers. If you do want to charge premium prices, what unique value are you offering to justify the higher cost?

Defining Your Market Positioning

Your restaurant's market positioning is essentially the unique space that you want to occupy in the minds of your target customers. This could be based on a variety of factors such as your quality of ingredients, culinary technique, serving size, customer service, or overall dining experience.

Once you've defined your market positioning, your pricing should align with it. For instance, if you position yourself as a budget-friendly eatery that delivers high-quality food, your prices need to reflect that. High prices may deter your target customer base, while low prices might signal a lack of quality. Conversely, if you're positioning yourself as a premium dining experience offering exotic ingredients and sophisticated recipes, your prices should be set higher to reflect the premium value you're delivering.

Think of your pricing as an extension of your restaurant's brand. It's not just about numbers; it's a communication tool that can convey your restaurant's value proposition and influence your customers' perceptions. By aligning your pricing with your market positioning, you can attract your desired customer base and build a strong brand identity in the virtual restaurant space.

However, bear in mind that regardless of your pricing strategy and market positioning, the quality and value you deliver must meet or exceed your customers' expectations. Overpricing can lead to disappointment, and underpricing can undermine your profitability. It's crucial to find a sweet spot that covers your costs, delivers value to your customers, and positions your virtual restaurant accurately in the marketplace.

8.3 Psychological Pricing Strategies

The way you structure your prices can greatly influence your customers' perception of value and their buying decisions. Psychological pricing strategies can be an effective tool in subtly guiding these decisions. By understanding how customers perceive and process prices, you can tweak your pricing structure in ways that make your offerings more attractive. Here are some common psychological pricing strategies you might consider implementing:

Charm Pricing

Also known as "just-below" pricing, this strategy involves reducing the price of an item by a small amount to make it appear significantly less expensive. For example, pricing an item at $9.99 instead of $10. This small change can make a big difference because customers often pay more attention to the number to the left of the decimal point and perceive $9.99 to be closer to $9 than $10.

Prestige Pricing

On the flip side, if you're positioning your virtual restaurant as a high-end dining experience, you might consider using prestige pricing. This strategy involves rounding prices up to the nearest whole number to convey a sense of quality and luxury. So, instead of selling a gourmet dish for $49.99, you might price it at $50 or even $55. This type of pricing strategy can enhance the perceived quality and value of your food.

Price Anchoring

Another powerful psychological pricing strategy is price anchoring. This involves listing a higher price next to the actual selling price of your item to highlight the value the customer is getting. For example, you could list the original price of a dish as $15, but offer it at a "discounted" price of $12. Seeing the higher original price first sets an anchor in the customer's mind, making the lower price seem like a great deal.

Bundle Pricing

Another strategy you can consider is bundle pricing, where you offer a set of items together at a lower price than if they were purchased separately. This not only provides perceived value to the customer but can also help you sell more items. For instance, offering a meal combo (main course, side, and drink) at a slightly lower price than the total of the individual items can encourage customers to order the combo instead of a single dish.

However, as you experiment with these psychological pricing strategies, it's essential to continuously monitor and evaluate their impact on your sales, profits, and customer perceptions. Different strategies may work better for different types of restaurants and customer segments, and it's important to find the one that best aligns with your business goals and brand identity.

Chapter 9. Customer Service in the Digital Age: Excellence in Every Interaction

The Importance of Digital Customer Service

In the digital landscape of the restaurant industry, customer service assumes a new level of complexity and importance. It moves beyond the tangible atmosphere and direct interpersonal interaction of a physical establishment and into a realm where the customer's entire dining experience is mediated by technology. In the absence of physical ambiance and face-to-face interaction, digital customer service becomes the principal avenue to create a lasting impression on your customers, and thus, is an area that demands a robust and well-considered approach.

A significant aspect of digital customer service in a virtual restaurant revolves around the ease and clarity of the order placing process. A well-structured, easy-to-navigate, and descriptive menu can enhance the customer's experience by eliminating confusion and facilitating a smooth transaction. Moreover, clear and enticing descriptions of each dish can whet the customer's appetite and increase the chances of repeat orders.

Promptness in communication also forms the backbone of excellent digital customer service. In the era of instant gratification, customers expect real-time assistance. A quick response to inquiries, acknowledgment of received orders, and providing updates about the preparation and delivery status of an order can make a customer feel valued and attended to.

In addition, integrating effective customer support channels such as live chat, email support, or even AI-powered chatbots can help address customer issues or complaints quickly and efficiently. Ensuring that customers have easy access to assistance when they face difficulties or have questions enhances their overall experience and satisfaction.

Receiving and acting upon customer feedback is another critical aspect of digital customer service. Whether positive or negative, every piece of feedback is an opportunity to refine your service and learn more about your customers' preferences. Demonstrating your responsiveness and dedication to continual improvement can turn even a critical customer into a loyal patron.

Lastly, remember that although the interaction is digital, the end service is deeply personal - providing a meal. Therefore, a touch of personalization can go a long way. This could be as simple as allowing customers to customize their orders or as thoughtful as sending personalized messages or offers on special occasions.

In summary, digital customer service in the realm of virtual restaurants should aim to create a seamless, enjoyable, and personalized experience for the customer. By focusing on clarity, prompt communication, effective problem resolution, receptiveness to feedback, and personal touches, you can leave a lasting impression on your customers and create a loyal customer base.

The Art of Communication

Mastering the art of communication can greatly enhance the quality of customer service your virtual restaurant provides. The words you use, the tone you adopt, and the speed at which you communicate can all influence a customer's perception of your brand and their overall dining experience. In a setting where physical interactions are nonexistent, effective communication becomes the primary tool to establish rapport, address concerns, and build a lasting relationship with your customers.

Firstly, clarity is essential when communicating about your dishes. This extends beyond simply stating what ingredients are in each dish. It involves conveying the taste, texture, preparation method, and even the inspiration behind each dish in a way that is appetizing and compelling. It means ensuring that any allergens are clearly marked, and that dietary preferences are catered to and clearly labeled. Miscommunication or lack of information can lead to unsatisfactory dining experiences and potentially serious health issues.

Response time is another key factor in effective communication. In the era of digital communication, customers often expect instant or near-instant responses. Prompt replies to inquiries or complaints not only resolve issues efficiently but also demonstrate your commitment to your customers' needs. Automated acknowledgments of inquiries can help manage expectations until a more personal response can be made. A good rule of thumb is to never leave a customer waiting for a response for more than 24 hours.

Navigating customer complaints and criticism requires careful and empathetic communication. It is crucial to listen actively to your customers' concerns, acknowledge their feelings, and provide a sincere apology if necessary. Avoid getting defensive; instead, focus on finding a solution to the issue and demonstrate your commitment to improving their experience. This helps to defuse negative situations and can turn a dissatisfied customer into a loyal one.

Your communication style should also be an extension of your brand identity. A playful brand might use casual, humorous language, while a high-end brand might opt for a more formal, polished tone. Consistency in your communication style helps reinforce your brand image and create a memorable brand personality.

However, no matter what your brand style, professionalism should always underpin your communications. Whether you are communicating with a happy customer or dealing with a complaint, maintaining a respectful, polite, and positive tone is imperative. Remember, every interaction with a customer is a reflection of your brand.

In conclusion, clear and accurate information, prompt responses, empathetic handling of feedback, a consistent communication style, and a professional tone are all crucial elements of the art of communication in customer service. By mastering these, you can enhance your customers' experience and cultivate a loyal customer base.

Handling Customer Complaints and Negative Feedback

Handling customer complaints and negative feedback is a crucial part of customer service, especially for virtual restaurants where word-of-mouth and online reviews can significantly impact business. It's not about if you will receive complaints, but when and how you respond to them. The art of handling complaints lies in prompt response, empathy, professionalism, effective problem-solving, and learning from the feedback.

Firstly, acknowledge that receiving complaints is a normal part of doing business. It's impossible to please every customer, and complaints provide valuable insight into areas where your service or product can improve. This shift in mindset can help to view complaints as opportunities for growth rather than negative events.

Prompt response is key. When customers voice their dissatisfaction, they want to be heard immediately. Delayed responses can exacerbate the situation, making customers feel ignored and increasing their frustration. Aim to respond within 24 hours, and sooner if possible. Even if you don't have an immediate solution, a quick acknowledgment can assure the customer that their concern is being taken seriously.

Empathy is crucial when dealing with upset customers. Customers want to feel that you understand and appreciate their feelings and viewpoint. Even if you don't agree with the customer's complaint, validate their feelings with statements like "I understand why you're upset," or "That sounds really frustrating." This can help to deescalate the situation and open up a productive dialogue.

Professionalism is another vital aspect. Even in the face of unjust or aggressive complaints, maintain a calm and respectful demeanor. Avoid becoming defensive or argumentative; instead, remain objective and focus on resolving the issue at hand. This can demonstrate your commitment to customer satisfaction and enhance your brand's reputation.

Effective problem-solving is the next step. Once you have listened and empathized, propose a solution to resolve the issue. This could be a refund, replacement, or another form of compensation, depending on the nature of the complaint. Keep in mind that the aim is not just to solve the problem but also to restore the customer's trust in your brand. This might sometimes mean going above and beyond the standard protocol.

Finally, use every complaint as a learning opportunity. Analyze each complaint to understand what went wrong and how you can prevent similar issues in the future. This could involve revising your menu descriptions, retraining your kitchen staff, or updating your delivery procedures.

Remember, a well-handled complaint can turn a negative situation into a positive one, potentially transforming a dissatisfied customer into a loyal advocate for your brand. Therefore, embrace complaints as valuable feedback, handle them with promptness, empathy, and professionalism, and continually improve your services based on the insights gained.

Leveraging Customer Reviews and Ratings

Customer reviews and ratings are the lifeblood of your online presence in the digital restaurant landscape. They serve as social proof of your restaurant's quality and can significantly impact your restaurant's reputation, visibility, and sales. By actively encouraging and managing these reviews, you can shape your online image and leverage this powerful form of digital word-of-mouth to your advantage.

The importance of positive reviews can't be overstated. Research indicates that consumers trust online reviews as much as personal recommendations from friends or family. Furthermore, high average ratings can improve your ranking on delivery platforms like DoorDash and make your restaurant more visible to potential customers. This can lead to increased orders and revenue.

To accumulate positive reviews, it's important to encourage your satisfied customers to share their experiences. This can be done through various ways:

1. **Direct requests:** At the end of a successful delivery, send a thank you message via the delivery platform or email, and ask them politely to leave a review.

2. **Incentives:** Offer small incentives, like discounts or freebies on their next order, for leaving a review.

3. **Social Media:** Encourage customers to leave reviews on your social media pages. This not only aids in collecting feedback but also helps in boosting your online presence.

While you aim for positive reviews, negative ones are inevitable. However, they provide a unique opportunity for improvement and damage control.

1. **Responding promptly:** Respond to negative reviews as quickly as possible. This demonstrates to the reviewer and other potential customers that you value their feedback and are committed to improving their experience.

2. **Acknowledgment and Apology:** Acknowledge the reviewer's concerns and apologize sincerely, regardless of whether the complaint is justified. This shows empathy and understanding, which can go a long way in soothing upset customers.

3. **Providing Solutions:** Offer a tangible solution to resolve the issue. This could be a refund, a redo of the order, or a discount on future orders. Showing that you're proactive in addressing complaints can help regain lost trust and may even convert a disgruntled customer into a loyal one.

4. **Taking Action:** Use negative reviews as constructive feedback. Analyze them to identify common issues or recurring complaints. Implement necessary changes in your operations to prevent similar complaints in the future, and consider letting the customer know what steps you've taken in response to their feedback.

In conclusion, customer reviews and ratings are powerful tools that, when used effectively, can enhance your reputation, improve your service, and drive your virtual restaurant's success. By actively encouraging positive reviews, responding to negative ones with empathy and professionalism, and continuously improving your offerings based on the feedback received, you can make the most of this digital word-of-mouth.

Ensuring a Seamless Delivery Experience

In a virtual restaurant landscape, the delivery experience can make or break a customer's impression of your restaurant. The journey from your kitchen to the customer's doorstep should be as smooth and as efficient as possible, ensuring that the food arrives in the same condition as it would be served in-house. Every aspect of this process, from packaging to the delivery partner, plays a crucial role in your overall customer service.

To begin with, let's discuss the importance of packaging. Proper packaging is not just about preventing spillage or leakage, although that certainly is a significant aspect. It's also about maintaining the optimal temperature of the food, preserving the freshness of the ingredients, and keeping the presentation intact. To ensure this:

1. **Material:** Use high-quality, sturdy packaging materials that can withstand the rigors of delivery without breaking or leaking.

2. **Insulation:** Consider thermally insulated packaging for temperature-sensitive dishes. For instance, hot meals may require foam containers, while cold dishes might be best served in sealed plastic containers.

3. **Compartmentalization:** Keep different food items separated to prevent cross-contamination or mixing of flavors. This is particularly important for dishes with sauces or gravies.

4. **Presentation**: While the functionality of packaging is crucial, don't overlook its aesthetics. Appealing, branded packaging can enhance the unboxing experience and elevate your restaurant's perceived value.

The next critical aspect is selecting a reliable delivery partner. With the rise of delivery platforms like DoorDash, it has become easier than ever to connect with independent delivery drivers. However, keep the following points in mind while working with them:

1. **Timeliness:** Aim to deliver within the promised timeframe. Punctuality is essential in the food delivery business. Late deliveries can result in cold food and unhappy customers.

2. Communication: Make sure your delivery partners understand the importance of keeping the customers updated about the delivery status, especially if there are unforeseen delays.

3. Professionalism: The delivery driver is the face of your restaurant during the delivery process. Hence, their demeanor, appearance, and professionalism should reflect the standards of your restaurant.

4. Care: The delivery drivers should handle the food packages with utmost care to maintain the quality of the food.

5. Feedback: Encourage your delivery partners to share feedback about customer reactions or any issues they faced during delivery. This frontline information can be incredibly valuable for improving your operations.

In conclusion, a seamless delivery experience is an integral part of digital customer service for virtual restaurants. By ensuring excellent packaging, partnering with reliable delivery personnel, and maintaining open lines of communication with your customers, you can elevate their experience from ordinary to extraordinary. Remember, every interaction with your customers contributes to their overall perception of your restaurant. By providing an exceptional delivery experience, you can leave a lasting positive impression, turning one-time customers into loyal patrons and advocates for your business.

Chapter 10: Strategies for Growth: Scaling Your Virtual Restaurant

Scaling your virtual restaurant involves expanding your operations, reaching new customers, and increasing revenue while maintaining or even improving the quality of your service and food. It's a complex process that requires careful planning, strategic decision-making, and diligent execution. This chapter will provide strategies for successfully growing your virtual restaurant business.

10.1 Streamlining Operations for Efficiency

In the context of scaling a virtual restaurant, operational efficiency is a critical aspect that directly affects the ability to handle increased demand without compromising the quality of food or service. Ensuring a seamless flow from the point of order to delivery is paramount, and achieving this requires diligent attention to the efficiency of all operational aspects of your restaurant.

Investing in Efficient Equipment

An effective way to streamline your operations is to invest in more efficient equipment. Commercial-grade kitchen appliances are designed for heavy-duty use and can significantly reduce cooking and preparation times. For example, a high-powered food processor can drastically cut down the time spent on chopping vegetables, while a commercial convection oven can cook food more quickly and evenly than a standard oven.

Consider the cost-benefit analysis of such investments. While the upfront costs may be high, the long-term gains in terms of time saved and increased capacity can more than make up for the initial expense. Remember, efficiency gains in the kitchen can translate directly into the ability to handle more orders, thereby boosting revenues.

Improving Food Preparation Systems

Improving your food preparation systems can have a significant impact on your operational efficiency. Consider implementing or refining your mise-en-place, the practice of preparing and organizing ingredients before the cooking process begins. This system ensures that everything you need for each dish is at hand when you need it, reducing the time wasted in searching for ingredients during cooking.

Another strategy could be batch preparation or cooking, where large quantities of a particular component are prepared at once. This is particularly effective for ingredients or dishes that keep well and are used across multiple menu items.

Optimizing Your Kitchen Layout

The layout of your kitchen plays a vital role in operational efficiency. A well-designed kitchen ensures a smooth workflow, minimizes unnecessary movements, and enhances safety.

Evaluate your current layout - is there a smooth flow from food storage to preparation areas, to the cooking line, and finally to the packaging area? Are frequently used tools and ingredients easily accessible? Do you have enough space to handle peak demand without the kitchen becoming overcrowded and chaotic?

If you identify problems in these areas, consider reorganizing your kitchen. This may involve rearranging equipment, setting up dedicated stations for different tasks, or even investing in remodeling your kitchen if necessary.

Regular Evaluation and Problem-Solving

Achieving operational efficiency is not a one-time task, but an ongoing process. Regularly evaluate your operations to identify bottlenecks and inefficiencies. This can involve observing your staff during peak times, timing how long different tasks take, or regularly asking your team for their input on what problems they're encountering.

Once you've identified issues, brainstorm solutions and implement them. Remember, the goal is continuous improvement. Small incremental changes can add up to significant efficiency gains over time.

Efficient operations are key to successfully scaling your virtual restaurant. By investing in efficient equipment, improving your food preparation systems, optimizing your kitchen layout, and continually seeking improvements, you can increase your capacity, speed up service times, and maintain the high quality that your growing customer base expects.

10.2 Expanding Your Menu

The prospect of menu expansion can be an exciting part of scaling up your virtual restaurant, serving the dual purpose of attracting a broader clientele and potentially increasing your average order value. Nevertheless, it is a delicate process that requires careful planning and execution to ensure consistency with your brand identity and maintain food quality.

Alignment with Your Brand

When considering what new items to introduce, remember that your menu is a direct reflection of your brand. Every dish should tell a part of your restaurant's story. Ask yourself - Does this new dish align with my brand? If your restaurant is positioned as a health-conscious eatery, adding a deep-fried, high-calorie item might not resonate with your target customers. Instead, opt for dishes that reinforce your brand identity, whether it's wholesome and healthy, globally inspired, or comfort food classics.

Maintaining Quality

As you expand your menu, never lose sight of the importance of quality. New dishes should meet the same high standards as your existing ones.

Carefully test each new dish multiple times, refining the recipe until it's just right. Rushing to add a plethora of new items without the proper vetting process can lead to a drop in overall quality, disappointing your customers and potentially damaging your reputation.

Efficient Use of Ingredients

Efficient use of ingredients is another critical consideration in menu expansion. Introducing new dishes that require a host of new ingredients can complicate inventory management and increase food waste. A smarter approach is to introduce dishes that utilize many of the same ingredients already in your inventory. This strategy, known as cross-utilization of ingredients, minimizes the need for additional storage space and reduces the risk of ingredients going unused.

Seasonal Dishes and Limited-Time Offers

Seasonal dishes and limited-time offers are a fantastic way to add variety and excitement to your menu. They provide an opportunity to showcase your creativity and keep your regular customers interested. Seasonal dishes, in particular, allow you to take advantage of fresh, locally available ingredients, which can improve the quality of your dishes and be a selling point for many customers.

Furthermore, limited-time offers can create a sense of urgency, encouraging customers to order before they miss out. They also offer a low-risk way to test new dishes. If a limited-time offer is well received, you might choose to add it to your regular menu.

Menu expansion is a balancing act between introducing new variety and maintaining operational efficiency and food quality. By ensuring new dishes align with your brand, maintaining your commitment to quality, intelligently managing your ingredients, and utilizing seasonal dishes or limited-time offers, you can effectively expand your menu as part of your growth strategy.

10.3 Leveraging Data for Decision-Making

In the digital era, the ability to gather and analyze data can be a game-changer for businesses, including virtual restaurants. Utilizing data allows you to make evidence-based decisions, which can significantly improve your restaurant's performance and profitability.

Sales Data

Sales data is a vital part of the puzzle. This includes information on your best-selling dishes, your busiest times, and your most valuable customers. This data can be used to make informed decisions on various aspects of your business.

For instance, if certain dishes are consistently outperforming others, you might consider featuring them more prominently on your menu or using them in promotional campaigns. Understanding your busiest times can help you manage staffing levels and food preparation schedules, ensuring you can meet demand while minimizing waste.

Also, identifying your most valuable customers — those who order frequently or spend more than average — can help you target your marketing efforts and loyalty programs. By recognizing and rewarding these customers, you can foster loyalty and potentially increase their lifetime value.

Customer Behavior and Preferences

In addition to sales data, understanding customer behavior and preferences can provide invaluable insights. This could involve analyzing trends in your reviews and ratings, surveying customers to gather feedback, or tracking how customers interact with your DoorDash page.

For example, if many customers leave comments praising a particular dish, you might consider featuring it more prominently or developing new dishes that feature the same popular ingredients or flavors. If you notice that customers are frequently asking questions about certain aspects of your menu or delivery options, you might need to provide more clarity in your descriptions or improve your communication.

Leveraging DoorDash Analytics

DoorDash provides powerful analytics tools that can help you delve deeper into your restaurant's performance and your customers' behaviors. These tools can offer insights into order trends, customer demographics, peak ordering times, and more.

For instance, if you see that a significant portion of your orders comes from a particular demographic group, you might consider tailoring your menu or marketing messages to appeal more to that group. Or, if you notice a drop in orders during a particular time of day, you might introduce special promotions to boost sales during that period.

Guiding Your Strategy

The insights derived from data can inform your growth strategies in a multitude of ways. They can guide your menu development, helping you understand which types of dishes to add or remove. They can inform your pricing strategies, showing you whether your prices are in line with what your customers are willing to pay. They can also guide your promotional campaigns, helping you understand what type of promotions are most effective and when they should be deployed.

Leveraging data in decision-making is a powerful strategy for growth. By analyzing and interpreting your sales data, understanding customer behavior and preferences, and using the analytics tools provided by DoorDash, you can make data-driven decisions that boost your restaurant's performance and set you on a path to successful growth.

10.4 Exploring New Marketing Channels

In a crowded virtual restaurant space, standing out is essential. A strategic approach to exploring and leveraging new marketing channels can be a potent tool in extending your restaurant's reach, driving customer acquisition, and building brand awareness.

Social Media Campaigns

In today's digital age, a robust social media presence is almost a necessity. It is a powerful tool to connect with your audience, share your story, and promote your offerings. Consider creating accounts on platforms popular with your target demographic, such as Instagram, Facebook, or TikTok.

Use these platforms to showcase your menu items through enticing photos or videos, introduce your kitchen staff, and share behind-the-scenes content that adds a personal touch. Regularly engage with your followers by responding to their comments, hosting contests, or asking for their input on new dishes.

In addition, social media platforms often have built-in tools for paid promotions. These tools allow you to target your advertisements based on factors like location, age, and interests, ensuring your promotions reach potential customers who are most likely to be interested in your restaurant.

Local Advertising

Depending on your target market, local advertising can also be a fruitful avenue. Consider placing ads in local newspapers, magazines, or radio stations. You can also explore options for outdoor advertising, such as billboards or transit ads.

When crafting your local advertisements, ensure they are clear, compelling, and reflective of your brand. Include a strong call to action – for instance, directing people to order through DoorDash – and consider offering special promotions to attract first-time customers.

Influencer Partnerships

Another increasingly popular marketing channel is influencer marketing. Partnering with social media influencers can boost your restaurant's visibility, particularly if the influencer's audience aligns with your target demographic.

Influencers can promote your virtual restaurant by posting about your dishes, sharing discount codes, or even collaborating on a special menu item. Just make sure to partner with influencers whose values align with your brand and who have a genuine connection with their followers for an authentic and effective promotion.

Local Business Partnerships

Last but not least, consider partnering with other local businesses. This could involve co-hosting events, cross-promoting each other's offerings, or creating special menu items that incorporate a partner's products. Such collaborations can help you tap into new customer bases and foster a sense of community.

In exploring new marketing channels, remember that it's not just about casting the net wide; it's also about making sure your message resonates with your audience. Tailoring your marketing strategies to your target audience's preferences and habits will lead to more effective outreach and ultimately, growth for your virtual restaurant. With a well-planned and executed marketing strategy, your restaurant will be well-positioned to attract new customers and keep regulars coming back for more.

10.5 Collaborating with DoorDash for Growth

DoorDash is more than just a delivery platform; it's a partner that can play an instrumental role in the growth and success of your virtual restaurant. The platform offers an array of features and programs designed to increase your restaurant's visibility, attract more customers, and enhance the overall customer experience. By strategically leveraging these offerings, you can effectively drive growth and scale your operations.

Participating in DoorDash Programs

One of the key programs offered by DoorDash is DashPass. DashPass is a subscription service where customers pay a monthly fee to receive reduced or waived delivery fees on their orders. Restaurants participating in DashPass often see an increase in orders because customers are incentivized to order more frequently from DashPass restaurants to maximize their subscription benefits.

Becoming a DashPass restaurant not only increases your visibility on the platform but also places you in a category of restaurants that customers are more likely to order from frequently. This could result in a significant boost in order volume and customer loyalty.

Maximizing Promotional Features

DoorDash's promotional features are another powerful tool for boosting your restaurant's growth. You have the ability to offer special deals or discounts, which DoorDash can highlight on their platform. These promotions can make your restaurant stand out amongst a sea of options, drawing in both new and existing customers.

Consider strategic timing for your promotions. For instance, offering a lunchtime special can help you capture more of the lunch crowd, while a weekend promotion might encourage larger orders for family meals.

Building a Strong Relationship with DoorDash

Forming a strong partnership with DoorDash can be beneficial to your virtual restaurant. Stay in regular communication with your DoorDash representative to stay updated on new features or opportunities.

Your representative can also provide valuable insights and advice tailored to your restaurant. This can include data on your performance, recommendations for improvements, or strategies to maximize your use of the platform.

Consider reaching out to DoorDash for support with promotional campaigns or menu optimization. Their expertise can help you devise effective growth strategies and navigate any challenges that arise.

Looking Ahead

The journey of growing your virtual restaurant is indeed exciting and, at times, challenging. But, by streamlining your operations, expanding your menu thoughtfully, making data-driven decisions, exploring new marketing channels, and harnessing the power of collaboration with DoorDash, you are setting your business up for success.

Remember, the customer is at the heart of your growth strategies. Their needs and expectations should be the guiding force behind every decision you make. As you scale, maintaining the essence of your brand and the quality of your food and service will be critical in turning first-time customers into loyal patrons. Keep pushing the boundaries, stay adaptable, and your virtual restaurant will thrive.

Chapter 11: Future of Virtual Restaurants: Trends to Watch Out for

As the food industry continues to evolve in the digital age, the landscape of virtual restaurants is set to transform in fascinating ways. Emerging technologies, changing consumer behaviors, and innovative business models are driving trends that are reshaping the concept of dining out. As a virtual restaurant owner, keeping an eye on these trends can equip you to seize new opportunities and stay ahead of the curve.

11.1 Technology Driving the Virtual Restaurant Experience

The continuous innovation in technology is set to revolutionize the virtual restaurant industry in various ways, impacting every aspect from operational efficiency and food delivery to the overall customer experience.

Artificial Intelligence and Machine Learning

Artificial Intelligence (AI) and machine learning are already transforming the landscape of various industries and the virtual restaurant sector is no exception. These technologies can analyze customer behavior and predict trends with remarkable accuracy.

For instance, by studying ordering patterns and preferences, AI can identify trends such as popular dishes during specific times or days. This can empower your restaurant to better manage inventory, ensuring you're sufficiently stocked with the ingredients for these popular dishes when demand is high, while also minimizing waste from overstocking less popular items.

Moreover, AI and machine learning can also personalize the marketing efforts of your restaurant. By analyzing customer preferences and dining habits, these technologies can help tailor promotional messages, special offers, and menu recommendations to individual customers, thereby enhancing customer engagement and boosting sales.

Advancements in Packaging Technology

In a virtual restaurant, the delivery experience is as crucial as the food itself. Advances in packaging technology promise to make significant improvements in this aspect.

Innovative packaging solutions can help maintain the temperature of food during transit, ensuring that hot dishes arrive hot, and cold items stay cool. They can also preserve the quality of food, preventing spillage or mix-ups, ensuring that food reaches customers in the intended state. Developments in eco-friendly packaging solutions also cater to the increasing consumer demand for sustainability.

Integration with Smart Home Technology

Another trend that is poised to make a significant impact on the virtual restaurant industry is the integration of restaurant services with smart home technology. As homes become smarter, with virtual assistants like Amazon's Alexa or Google's Home becoming commonplace, customers might soon be able to place their food orders directly via these devices.

For instance, a customer might be able to say, "Alexa, order my favorite pasta from XYZ Restaurant," without having to manually navigate an app or website. This seamless integration could make the ordering process even more convenient and efficient for customers, enhancing their overall experience.

By staying abreast of these technology trends and adopting relevant innovations, your virtual restaurant can continuously enhance its operations, service, and customer experience, thereby ensuring its competitiveness in the evolving industry landscape.

11.2 Evolution of Consumer Preferences

Understanding the evolving consumer preferences is vital for the continued success and growth of any business, and the virtual restaurant industry is no exception. The choices customers make are increasingly influenced by several factors including health-consciousness, sustainability, and culinary curiosity, to name a few. Keeping an eye on these trends can help shape your restaurant's strategy for the future.

Health-Conscious Dining

More and more people are becoming conscious of their diet and nutritional intake. This shift towards healthier lifestyles is driving a significant change in the food industry. There is a growing demand for wholesome, nutritious, and well-balanced meals that do not compromise on taste.

In response to this trend, many virtual restaurants are increasingly incorporating health-focused options in their menus. From offering dishes with more fruits, vegetables, and whole grains, to providing low-calorie or low-carb options, to catering to specific dietary preferences like vegan, gluten-free, or keto diets - there are various ways to cater to the health-conscious consumer. Virtual restaurants that can deliver on taste while promoting good health are likely to see an uptick in popularity and customer loyalty.

Sustainability as a Priority

Sustainability is another influential trend in the food and restaurant industry. Today's consumers are more environmentally conscious and often make dining decisions based on the eco-friendly practices of a restaurant. This trend is set to shape the future of the virtual restaurant industry in a big way.

This could manifest in various aspects of your restaurant's operations. Sourcing ingredients locally not only reduces carbon emissions associated with long-distance transportation but also supports local farmers and suppliers. Using biodegradable or reusable packaging for food delivery can reduce waste and environmental impact. Implementing efficient food preparation methods can help minimize food waste.

Transparently communicating these sustainable practices to your customers can enhance your restaurant's image and appeal to eco-conscious consumers.

Culinary Diversity and Experimentation

Another interesting trend is the growing consumer interest in exploring diverse and exotic cuisines. As customers become more adventurous with their food choices, they seek new, unique culinary experiences. Virtual restaurants offering an array of world cuisines, fusion dishes, or novel food concepts are likely to attract these gastronomic explorers.

Staying tuned to these evolving consumer preferences and aligning your virtual restaurant accordingly can help you stay ahead of the competition and ensure the continued growth and success of your restaurant.

11.3 Innovations in Business Models

The virtual restaurant landscape is ripe for innovation, and the future may see the emergence of creative business models that push the boundaries of traditional food service. As these trends unfold, they could offer exciting opportunities for virtual restaurant operators. Here's a more detailed look at what some of these trends might entail:

Hybrid Models

Hybrid models that merge the traditional dine-in experience with a virtual restaurant operation could become more commonplace. This model allows businesses to maximize their revenue streams by catering to both in-person diners and online customers. It can help a restaurant reach a wider customer base, catering to those who prefer the ambiance and experience of dining out, as well as those who prefer the convenience of delivery.

For instance, a restaurant could operate as a typical dine-in establishment during peak meal times, then switch to a delivery-only model during off-peak hours. This approach could help optimize kitchen operations, making the most of staff and resources.

Multiple Brands under One Roof

The concept of 'ghost kitchens' hosting multiple virtual brands is gaining traction. This model enables restaurant operators to run several virtual brands from a single kitchen, each focusing on a different cuisine or dining experience.

This strategy allows operators to diversify their offerings without significantly increasing operational costs or complexity. For instance, a single kitchen could potentially operate a burger joint, a salad bar, and a sushi place all under different virtual brands. This approach allows a business to cater to a wide variety of customer preferences and boost its overall order volume.

Collaborations and Partnerships

The future might see more collaborations and partnerships in the virtual restaurant space. Restaurants could team up with influencers or celebrity chefs to create signature dishes or even whole menus, drawing in fans and adding a touch of star power to their offerings.

Similarly, collaborations between restaurants themselves could become more common. By combining their culinary strengths, two or more restaurants could create unique fusion dishes or limited-time menu specials that provide customers with an exclusive dining experience.

Exclusive Delivery Partnerships

As the competition among food delivery platforms intensifies, some virtual restaurants might choose to form exclusive partnerships with specific delivery services. Such arrangements could offer strategic benefits like increased visibility on the delivery platform's app or website, priority ranking in search results, or more favorable terms such as lower commission rates.

This approach can help a restaurant build a strong brand presence on a particular platform, potentially driving more orders. However, it's important for restaurants to weigh these benefits against the risk of limiting their reach by not being available on other popular delivery platforms.

In conclusion, the future of the virtual restaurant industry is set to be dynamic and exciting, driven by ongoing innovations in technology, shifting consumer preferences, and new business models. Staying informed and adaptable in the face of these changes will be key to navigating the path ahead successfully.

Chapter 12: Conclusion: The Recipe for Your DoorDash Success

As we wrap up this guide, it is crucial to reiterate that operating a successful virtual restaurant on DoorDash is as much about culinary creativity as it is about business acumen. By keeping abreast of industry trends, honing your operational efficiency, delivering excellent customer service, and leveraging the robust features of DoorDash, you can not only set up your restaurant for success but also sustain it in the long run.

12.1 Consolidating Your Learning

As we reach the end of this guide, it is time to consolidate and reflect upon the wealth of knowledge that we've encountered throughout this journey. The road to establishing a prosperous virtual restaurant via DoorDash is multi-faceted and involves several key areas of understanding and practice.

Understanding the Concept and Benefits of a Virtual Restaurant

We began our exploration by comprehending the idea and the many advantages of a virtual restaurant. Virtual restaurants are delivery-only establishments that operate from a commercial kitchen with no physical dining area. They are also referred to as ghost kitchens, cloud kitchens, or dark kitchens. They allow for lower operational costs, increased flexibility, and quick adaptation to trends, while also providing a sustainable way to explore new culinary concepts with minimized risk.

The Role of DoorDash

In Chapter 2, we dove into understanding DoorDash as a platform - its purpose, advantages, and how it facilitates the operation of virtual restaurants. DoorDash, as one of the leading food delivery platforms, offers exposure to a vast customer base, effective promotional tools, and valuable data analytics to assist in your business decisions. Its robust infrastructure and user-friendly interface make it a preferred choice for both restaurant owners and customers.

Strategies for Pricing, Customer Service, Delivery Logistics, and Marketing

In subsequent chapters, we elaborated on various strategies essential for a successful virtual restaurant. These strategies encompassed pricing your menu right considering the food cost and profit margins, providing exceptional digital customer service, managing delivery logistics for a seamless customer experience, and effective marketing practices to enhance your visibility and appeal on the DoorDash platform.

Maintaining a Growth Mindset and Being Receptive to Evolving Trends

Lastly, we emphasized the importance of having a growth mindset. This includes consistently evaluating and improving your operations, expanding your offerings, making data-informed decisions, and exploring new marketing channels. We also discussed the significance of being open to innovations and staying updated with evolving industry trends, be it in technology, consumer preferences, or new business models.

Reflecting on these key areas provides a comprehensive understanding of the virtual restaurant industry and how to navigate it successfully via DoorDash. It is important to remember that while this guide offers a structured approach, the practical application of these insights will require customization based on your unique circumstances and continuous fine-tuning based on your experience.

12.2 Tailoring Your Approach

As we've stressed throughout this guide, the restaurant industry, and more specifically, the virtual restaurant sector, is a dynamic and continuously evolving field. Therefore, while the strategies and insights shared in this guide provide a solid foundation, it is essential to understand that there isn't a 'one-size-fits-all' solution when it comes to operating a successful virtual restaurant on DoorDash. The strategy that works for one restaurant may not work for another. As such, you must tailor your approach according to your unique circumstances and offerings.

Recognize Your Unique Strengths

Every virtual restaurant has its distinct characteristics and strengths, be it the type of cuisine, cooking methods, unique recipes, sustainability practices, branding, or the use of locally-sourced ingredients. Identifying these unique strengths is the first step to carving out a niche for yourself in the crowded virtual restaurant space. Leverage these strengths in your menu creation, marketing messages, and customer service practices.

Understand Your Target Audience

The customers you aim to serve will significantly influence how you run your virtual restaurant. Their preferences, dietary restrictions, budget, ordering patterns, and feedback are invaluable inputs to customize your approach. Understanding your target audience helps in making decisions about menu items, pricing, promotional offers, and even your communication style.

Stay Adaptable and Open to Experimentation

The most successful virtual restaurants are those that are adaptable and responsive to changes. This could mean pivoting your menu to accommodate a new food trend, adopting a new technology to enhance the ordering experience, or tweaking your operations to improve efficiency. Experimentation is crucial. Whether it's A/B testing different marketing messages or trialing new dishes, be open to learning from these experiments to refine your strategies.

Use Data to Guide Your Decisions

As you operate your restaurant, you'll accumulate a wealth of data - from customer order histories to peak times for orders, popular dishes, and customer feedback. This data is a treasure trove of insights that can inform your decisions and help you tailor your strategies more effectively.

In conclusion, the road to success in the virtual restaurant industry is paved with a deep understanding of your unique strengths, a keen knowledge of your target audience, a readiness to adapt and experiment, and a data-driven mindset. By embracing these principles, you can set your virtual restaurant up for success and longevity in the ever-evolving DoorDash ecosystem.

12.3 The Importance of Persistence

Building a prosperous virtual restaurant on DoorDash, much like any business venture, is not an endeavor that yields immediate results. It's a journey marked by constant learning, adapting, and growing. This path to success demands a level of patience, determination, and most importantly, persistence that can sometimes be challenging but is ultimately rewarding.

Patience in Building Your Brand

In the fast-paced world of digital platforms, it may seem like success should be instantaneous. However, building a strong brand and a loyal customer base takes time. It involves meticulously crafting your brand identity, consistently delivering quality service, and gradually winning over customers with your exceptional offerings. Remember, every interaction, every dish, and every customer review contributes to the reputation of your restaurant. Patience is key in allowing your brand to mature and come into its own.

Determination Amidst Challenges

In your journey as a virtual restaurant owner, you'll undoubtedly face a variety of challenges. From handling customer complaints, dealing with supply chain issues, to facing competition, these hurdles can be demanding. It's your determination and resilience in the face of these adversities that will keep your restaurant afloat and advancing. Instead of becoming disheartened, use these challenges as catalysts to strengthen your problem-solving skills and improve your operations.

Persistence in the Face of Setbacks

Setbacks are inevitable in any business. There might be times when a new menu item doesn't receive the response you'd hoped for, a marketing campaign falls flat, or a tough review affects your rating. While these instances can be discouraging, they are not definitive of your restaurant's potential. It's important to persist despite these setbacks. View them as feedback and opportunities to learn, adapt, and improve. Use them to fine-tune your strategies and continuously better your offerings and services.

Consistency in Delivering Quality

Regardless of the challenges and setbacks, maintaining consistency in delivering high-quality food and service is paramount. Customers value and trust brands that deliver consistently, and this can be a significant differentiator for your restaurant.

In summary, establishing a thriving virtual restaurant on DoorDash is a marathon, not a sprint. It requires not just a sound strategy and a great concept, but also patience to let your brand grow, determination to overcome challenges, persistence to keep moving forward despite setbacks, and consistency in delivering quality. Keep these values at the core of your operations, and you'll be well on your way to realizing your restaurant's potential and achieving long-term success.

12.4 Staying Customer-Centric

At the core of any successful business lies an unerring focus on the customer. This becomes even more vital in the realm of virtual restaurants, where direct, in-person interactions are replaced by digital interfaces, and customer experiences are defined by different parameters. Therefore, it is essential to infuse a customer-centric approach in all aspects of your virtual restaurant business. Here's how you can stay customer-centric:

Understanding Your Customers

The first step in staying customer-centric is having a profound understanding of who your customers are, what they value, and what their expectations are. This includes knowledge of their dining preferences, dietary restrictions, preferred order times, and more. DoorDash's data analytics can provide valuable insights into customer behavior, which can be leveraged to create personalized experiences that resonate with them. By understanding your customers' needs and preferences, you can curate offerings that are most likely to satisfy them.

Prioritizing Customer Satisfaction

Customer satisfaction should be a top priority for your virtual restaurant. This goes beyond just serving great food. It encompasses every interaction a customer has with your restaurant, from browsing the menu and placing an order to receiving their meal and providing feedback. Each of these touchpoints is an opportunity to delight your customers. Clear and attractive menu descriptions, easy ordering processes, prompt delivery, and responsive customer service all contribute to a positive customer experience.

Valuing Customer Feedback

In the digital age, customers have a powerful voice. Reviews and ratings can significantly influence a restaurant's online reputation. Treat every piece of feedback as a precious resource. Positive reviews acknowledge what you're doing right, and constructive criticism highlights areas for improvement. Respond to all reviews in a timely and respectful manner. Thank customers for their compliments and assure them that their suggestions or complaints are taken seriously and will be addressed.

Building Customer Loyalty

Beyond just satisfying your customers, strive to earn their loyalty. Loyal customers are more likely to order from your restaurant regularly, spend more per order, and recommend your restaurant to others, driving your growth. Foster loyalty by consistently exceeding customer expectations, personalizing their experiences, and rewarding them for their patronage. Consider loyalty programs or special offers for regular customers.

In conclusion, a customer-centric approach is the cornerstone of a successful virtual restaurant. Remember, you are not merely in the business of selling food; you are in the business of creating exceptional dining experiences. Keep your customers at the heart of everything you do, and success is sure to follow.

12.5 Your Journey Awaits: Embrace the Adventure

Every new venture carries with it a sense of adventure, and starting a virtual restaurant on DoorDash is no different. You are setting foot into a rapidly evolving landscape of food delivery, joining a digital revolution that has redefined the way we think about food and dining. This journey may be filled with learning, experimenting, adapting, and innovating. Embrace these opportunities with open arms, for each step brings you closer to realizing your vision.

The Joy of Sharing Your Culinary Creations

One of the most rewarding aspects of running a virtual restaurant is the ability to share your culinary creations with a wide and diverse audience. Each dish you serve is a testament to your culinary passion and craftsmanship. It's an expression of your creativity and dedication that gets to be part of your customers' celebrations, comfort, and daily life. This realization brings an immense sense of satisfaction and fulfillment.

Being Part of Customers' Lives

As a virtual restaurant owner, you play a crucial role in your customers' lives. Your dishes might be the highlight of a family dinner, the comfort food for someone having a tough day, or the centerpiece of a celebration. You have the opportunity to create delightful experiences and lasting memories for your customers, making this journey truly rewarding.

Carving Your Own Success Story

Each decision you make, each strategy you implement, and each milestone you achieve is a chapter in your unique DoorDash success story. This guide has given you the tools and insights to start writing that story, but how it unfolds is entirely up to you. Be patient with your progress, celebrate your achievements, learn from your setbacks, and never lose sight of your vision.

Embracing the Future

The future of the restaurant industry is digital, and by launching your virtual restaurant on DoorDash, you're positioning yourself at the forefront of this evolution. This journey is an exciting one, filled with opportunities to grow, innovate, and succeed. So gear up and take that first step on your DoorDash adventure today.

In conclusion, success in the world of virtual restaurants is a blend of many ingredients: a strong concept, an appealing menu, efficient operations, exceptional customer service, strategic marketing, and an unwavering commitment to your customers. This guide has aimed to equip you with the knowledge and strategies you need to combine these ingredients effectively. Now, it's your turn to start cooking up your DoorDash success story. Bon appétit and best of luck on your journey!

www.ingramcontent.com/pod-product-compliance
Lightning Source LLC
Chambersburg PA
CBHW031445210526
45464CB00005B/2338